Using little more than two hands and a rolling pin, anyone can become a *sfoglino* with this comprehensive guide to the handmade pasta of Emilia-Romagna.

American Sfoglino shows you how to make this incredible pasta at home.

Exploring 15 pasta shapes, chef Evan Funke provides meticulous instruction and step-by-step photography for each stage of the process. From the fundamentals of pasta dough and rolling *sfoglia* with precision to the right way to blanch, dry, and preserve pasta, Funke provides a master class within these pages.

Evan Funke is a true *American Sfoglino*. After an apprenticeship at La Vecchia Scuola Bolognese and decades in restaurant kitchens, Funke has mastered the old-world techniques of handmade pasta and brought his craft to Felix Trattoria in Los Angeles, captivating diners with unforgettable dishes. Each plate is a reflection of the culinary traditions of Emilia-Romagna. Honed and evolved through Funke's distinctive lens, his dishes have earned the reputation of best pasta in America.

With recipes for rich bowls of **Tortelloni Burro e Oro**, plates of **Tagliatelle in Bianco con Proscuitto**, and **Lasagna Verde alla Bolognese**, along with stories from Emilia-Romagna, Funke brings the art and pleasure of handmade pasta home.

AMERICAN
SFOGLINO

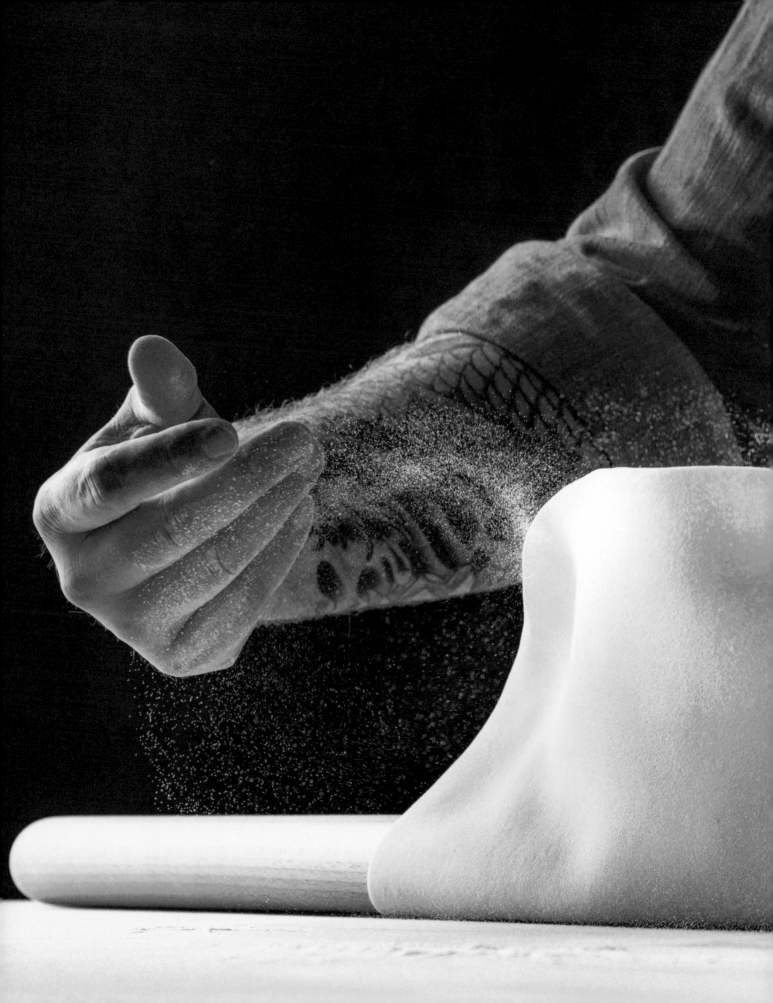

ERICAN
OGLINO

A Master Class
in Handmade Pasta

EVAN FUNKE
with **Katie Parla**

Photographs by **Eric Wolfinger**
Foreword by **Nancy Silverton**

CHRONICLE BOOKS
SAN FRANCISCO

For Grace

Library of Congress Cataloging-in-Publication Data:

Names: Funke, Evan, author. | Parla, Katie, author. | Wolfinger, Eric, photographer.
Title: American sfoglino : a master class in handmade pasta / by Evan Funke
    with Katie Parla ; photographs by Eric Wolfinger.
Description: San Francisco : Chronicle Books, [2019] | Includes index.
Identifiers: LCCN 2018059142 | ISBN 9781452173313 (hardcover : alk. paper)
Subjects: LCSH: Cooking (Pasta) | Cooking, Italian.
Classification: LCC TX809.M17 F86 2019 | DDC 641.82/2—dc23
    LC record available at https://lccn.loc.gov/2018059142

Design by Vanessa Dina.

Typesetting by Jared Gentz.

Manufactured in China.

Chronicle books and gifts are available at special quantity discounts to corporations,
professional associations, literacy programs, and other organizations. For details and
discount information, please contact our premiums department at corporatesales@
chroniclebooks.com or at 1-800-759-0190.

Chronicle Books LLC
680 Second Street
San Francisco, California 94107
www.chroniclebooks.com

MIX
Paper from
responsible sources
FSC™ C008047
FSC
www.fsc.org

10 9 8 7 6 5 4 3 2 1

I once told my sister that Evan Funke managed to do something old friends and even the Pacific Ocean haven't been able to do. He managed to get me west of the 405 Freeway, the insurmountable L.A. traffic barrier, to his restaurant Felix, that temple of pasta and other wonderful foods served about a half mile from the funkiness of the Venice Beach Boardwalk. In *American Sfoglino*, Evan goes one step further as he brings Venice—and Bologna—right to your own kitchen.

Evan is a true American *sfoglino*. But he wasn't born into it. Being a *sfoglino* didn't come from his roots, it wasn't passed down to him through generations of his family. In fact, if you didn't know who he was, you'd likely think he was more suited as a Hells Angel than a pasta master. Look at the forearms on the guy. They've got more ink than the Monday edition of the *Los Angeles Times*.

Evan's identity as a *sfoglino* has come through apprenticeship and dedication. He searched out a master. Actually, in his quest, he was fortunate enough to learn from two masters. One is "The Maestra" Alessandra Spisni, a legend in Bologna and eight-time world champion pasta maker. The other is Kosaku Kawamura, a Japanese master who taught Evan the freedom to go beyond traditional methodology.

In *American Sfoglino*, Evan honors this rigorous training from two of the most influential pasta makers in the world and passes it on to you. Hopefully, you'll pass it along, too.

As a chef and author who has spent the past 40 years obsessing over the details of my craft, I can recognize singular dedication and value. This book might just be the finest, most educational tool available about the art of fresh pasta making. The first section contains essential master doughs and all the fundamentals, a culmination of Evan's years of training and experience in those pages. Read and reread this section, as I will, then practice its lessons and practice some more. I know you'll be tempted to jump in and start making your own pasta, but please read the details before attempting to recreate those beautiful dishes.

Thanks to Evan's maniacal enthusiasm, you may never again be tempted to buy dried, packaged pasta at the supermarket. And before you know it, the word *sfoglino* will roll off your tongue as expertly as you roll *sfoglia* itself.

—NANCY SILVERTON

SFOGLIA

(sfol-EE-a):

A sheet of hand-rolled fresh pasta dough.

SFOGLINO or SFOGLINA

(sfol-YEE-no or sfol-YEE-na):

A maker of fresh pasta sheets.

Being a *sfoglino*, or pasta maker, in Bologna is a position of honor, deeply rooted in the city's cultural history, traditions, and lore. For hundreds of years, bolognese pasta makers have practiced their daily ritual of rolling pasta by hand in *laboratori* (workshops) and homes all over the city. *Sfoglini* are the very foundation of bolognese cuisine.

My acquaintance with *sfoglini* and their craft began more than a decade ago, at the tail end of 2007. I was stuck in a dead-end job at a shitty hotel in Beverly Hills. I felt completely lost. While battling bouts of hopelessness, a singular thought struck me one day and it would, ultimately, change my entire life: I wanted to make pasta by hand. To achieve this goal, I wanted the best teacher in Italy (therefore, the world). In those days, the internet was not what it is today—think: dial up and web pages. After scouring the web for months, I stumbled across a page with a link to La Vecchia Scuola Bolognese run by a woman named Alessandra Spisni. Through a series of emails and phone calls in broken Italian, I eventually secured a position as a student.

Via Malvasia 49, the original location of La Scuola, was 5 kilometers [about 3 miles] from my little apartment on Via Stalingrado. Each day, I hoofed it from that apartment in Bologna's red-light district to the school and back, and everywhere in between. Back then La Vecchia Scuola Bolognese was a tiny ground-level *laboratorio* with a shoebox kitchen and a 12-table private dining room. Alessandra was not yet the powerhouse celebrity chef she is today, but she was surely impressive. She was a teacher, a mother, a cook, and Emilia-Romagna's preeminent

sfoglina. Over the next three months, she would lovingly bestow upon me the fundamentals of making *sfoglia*—sheets of pasta rolled with a rolling pin called a *mattarello*. Included in these lessons was a veritable master class in the richness of the bolognese kitchen.

During my pivotal stay in Bologna I also encountered another masterful character, Kosaku Kawamura, who opened my mind to a different perspective, one that allowed me to see past some of the dogma surrounding Italian culinary traditions. The fundamentals that lie herein are a confluence of these two perspectives and define this book.

Much like the traditions passed on here, pasta making is cumulative. This book is a distillation of my time in Bologna, followed by 10 years of trial and error, curiosity, and repetition. The skills and stories in these pages represent hundreds of years of practical knowledge and the people and philosophies that have shaped my understanding of bolognese traditions. It is my responsibility as a perpetual student and custodian of these traditions and techniques to pass on to you what I have learned.

I've been chasing a seemingly unattainable balance between texture and structure, elasticity and extensibility, heart and mind. I am chasing the perfect *sfoglia* and, maybe, through the fundamentals in this book, with some perseverance and love, you can find yours, too.

Maestra
Alessandra Spisni

When I rang the doorbell at La Vecchia Scuola for the first time, I was greeted by a broad shouldered woman clad in a flower print smock. Alessandra Spisni bellowed, "*BUONGIORNO*," in the singsong sway of the bolognesi. At first glance, the eight-time world champion of *La Sfoglia d'Oro* competition was intimidating to say the least, but I was immediately enamored of her gentle nature and generosity.

A pasta maker since the age of six, Alessandra embodies the soul of the *sfoglina*. When you watch her roll *sfoglia*, it's like a dance in which each partner is intimately aware of the movements and tempo, but understands the dance is never the same. "*Piano, piano, in harmonia*," she would say while instructing her students—in harmony and with patience. Another lesson that stuck with me is "*perchè la sfoglia non è sempre uguale*"—the pasta sheet isn't always the same. The *maestra* showed me a true sense of harmony in pasta making that can only be discovered through practice and patience. I feel so fortunate to be a student of Alessandra's. Her command of the bolognese kitchen and innate ability with the *mattarello* made a monumental impression on me. Her love and patience are what guide me today and what I offer you in this book. Aside from Lee Hefter, of Spago Beverly Hills, Alessandra stands alone as the single most influential figure of my career.

Kosaku Kawamura, Japanese Sfoglino

Kosaku Kawamura, in my opinion, is technically the best *sfoglino* in the world. He is *shokunin* (master craftsman). He is an ardent and astute practitioner of handmade pasta. When I met Ko at La Scuola, our friendship was immediate. We recognized in each other the pursuit of perfection. He opened my eyes to the ingenious natural engineering of the shapes of pasta and asked me to look beyond tradition and explore a more systematic approach to pasta making. Knowing my own uncompromising nature, it was no surprise his philosophy was hugely influential.

Base, Ko's miniscule *laboratorio* and dining room in the Bunkyo-ku area of Tokyo, sits across the street from a police station. Outside, a sign reads: *NON SI MANGIA BENE QUI*—you will not eat well here. There is no waitstaff, nor menu. There is just Ko and his tagliatelle *in bianco*, tender strands of pasta dressed with oil and Parmigiano-Reggiano. A brusque challenge is issued to each customer upon arrival. Kosaku is serious about his profession and wants to know if you are serious, too. His kitchen is simple— just a two-burner stove, a sink, and a refrigerator for the beer. If you are lucky enough to sit at one of the eight stools, you can witness the deft precision of his preparation. Each portion of tagliatelle is preciously wrapped in absorbent towels. He uses a matcha brush to quickly emulsify a splash of pasta water and olive oil in a plastic bowl while the tagliatelle swims in a bath of delicately seasoned water. Kosaku's pasta is supremely balanced. Much like a perfect grain of sushi rice, each strand of tagliatelle is unique on the palate. A quick dusting of Parmigiano-Reggiano and a crack of black pepper are the only adornments.

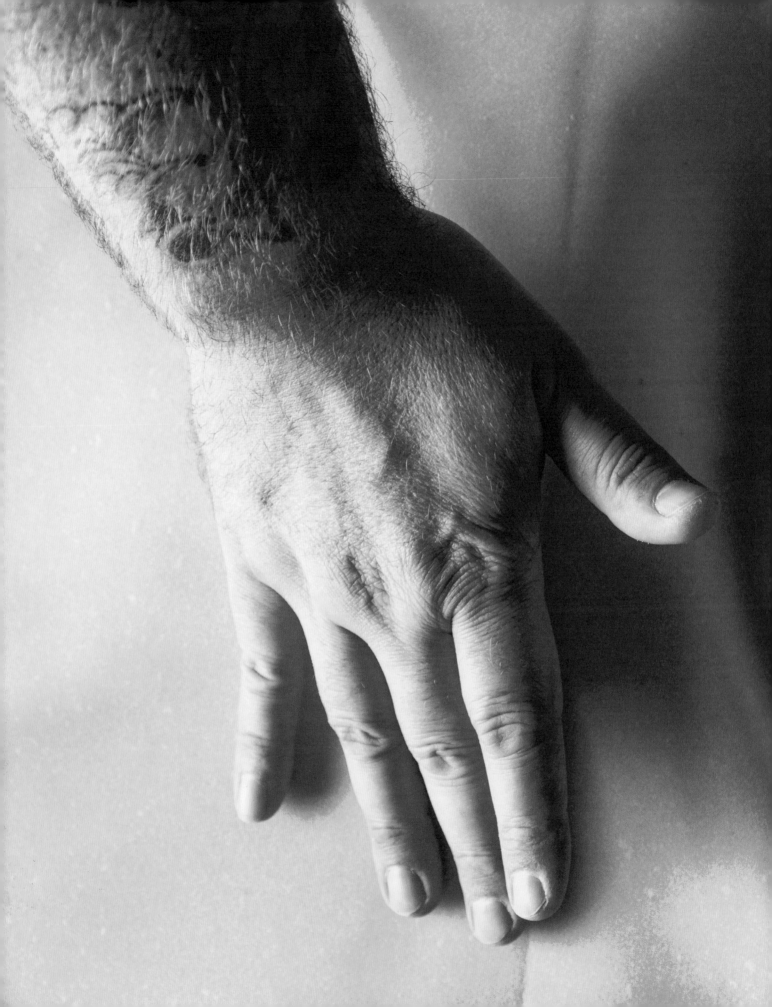

PART 1:
FUNDAMENTALS

The Basics

The recipes in this book include traditional, centuries-old pasta forms such as Tagliatelle (page 84) and Lasagna (page 64), as well as some creative ones Maestra Alessandra invented during her days as a *sfoglina*, such as the Smeraldine (page 184).

Each of the 14 pasta shapes included here has been chosen for both its process and history. In accordance with the customs of Bologna, pasta shapes are paired with specific sauces.

Always read the entire recipe before beginning to cook. Some recipes require time-sensitive prep work, which is mentioned in the recipe's headnote.

Here's what you need to know to make handmade pasta. *Andiamo*!

Measurements

The Master Dough recipes are written in grams and I insist you use them as intended. The metric system is the most reliable measurement scale for achieving the most consistent final product in the kitchen and I use it for **both** liquid and dry ingredients.

Non-dough recipes are written in pounds and by volume, as needed, with metric equivalents.

Fuck your Pasta Machine

A *sfoglia*, the heart of this book, is a sheet of pasta rolled by hand. Some people form it with a pasta machine. If you follow me on Instagram (@evanfunke), you already know my feelings on that (#fuckyourpastamachine). In my experience, nothing beats a *sfoglia* hand-rolled with a *mattarello*. For more on this, see page 26.

Dough Yields

I've developed each Master Dough recipe, with the exception of Gnocchi di Ricotta (page 46), to yield between 710 to 770 g [a bit over 1½ lb] of dough, which serves about 6 people. Most home kitchens can't accommodate a very large sheet of pasta, so I recommend halving the dough and rolling out two *sfoglie*.

If you're tempted to cut the dough recipe in half because you are serving fewer than 6 people (or don't want leftovers), let me talk you out of it. A batch of dough smaller than 700 g [about 1½ lb] is more difficult to knead and doesn't develop the ideal gluten network as easily. If rolling and shaping so much pasta is daunting, invite some friends. And if you don't have any, a great way to make some is by offering fresh pasta! You don't need to roll out and cook all the pasta at once. The dough will keep, tightly wrapped in the refrigerator, for up to 4 days.

Single Thickness

When cooked, most pastas that involve a fold (for instance, *strichetti*, *triangoli*, or *tortelloni*) tend to have thick and crunchy, or chewy, parts. That's because there are multiple connection points where the pasta is at double or more thickness. However, by pressing these points to a single layer—or "single thickness"—you eliminate thicker sections, thereby ensuring even and uniform texture.

Batches

Ragù is one of those things, like a soup or stew, that bolognesi never make in small quantities. It's best made in large amounts, which is why the ragù recipes in this book yield enough for 2 or 3 batches of pasta. I like having extra sauce on hand, especially when it will keep, in airtight containers, in the refrigerator for up to 1 week, or in the freezer for up to 6 months. That said, if you aren't a fan of leftovers, you *can* scale down the ragù recipes.

Salting the Water

When seasoning water in which to boil pasta or vegetables, add enough salt so it tastes like a seasoned soup (a good guideline is 3½ Tbsp [55 g] salt to 8 qt [7.5 L] water). This level of salinity will lend key flavor to whatever you are cooking, especially considering salted pasta water is used in some recipes to make an emulsified sauce.

Cooking Pasta

Remember, fresh pasta cooks much faster than dried and there's not as much leeway in the cooking time. It can overcook quickly, so it's important to stay nearby and taste often. When the pasta has lost its raw bite and is tender, but not yet soft, remove it from the water immediately. And, in case you're wondering, fresh pasta cannot be cooked to "al dente" because it was never hard to begin with.

Pairing Shapes and Sauces

In keeping with bolognese custom, I've paired each of the book's pasta shapes with one or more specific sauces. The combinations are classic and central to Bologna's pasta traditions.

There's an entire philosophy behind these matches, guided by local tradition and textural harmony. The quintessential example is Tagliatelle al Ragù della Vecchia Scuola (page 90). In Bologna, there are few chances of finding the city's famed meat sauce paired with any other pasta shape. The whole city agrees: the sauce clings more perfectly to the long, thin egg-based strands than any alternative. I'm not saying don't experiment; I do and I also expect you will. But learning and appreciating the basics and tradition first is important for establishing a base of knowledge.

The Sfoglino's Arsenal–Equipment and Ingredients

In Bologna, with few exceptions, *sfoglini* are either professional pasta makers or they are *nonne* who make pasta for their families. Both are dedicated to preserving the city's pasta traditions, and while their output may vary–you make a lot more pasta as a *sfoglino* for a pasta shop or restaurant than you ever would for even the largest bolognese family–their tools are the same.

To roll *sfoglia* by hand, you need the same special tools *sfoglini* bolognesi depend on. Following is a list of essentials to help you bring the spirit of the city's cooking into your home. (The tools are grouped by process and in the order they will be used.)

EQUIPMENT

MEASURING AND STORING

The thousands of *nonne* in Bologna who keep the fresh pasta tradition alive never measure–much less weigh–their ingredients. But their pasta expertise is the product of decades of trial and error. They've developed a finely honed touch memory and can intuitively adjust pasta dough on the fly. Until you get to that point, throw down $10 for a **digital scale** that weighs ingredients in grams. It's the quickest and most accurate way to make the best dough possible. Also, stock **plastic wrap** for wrapping dough balls.

ROLLING

In Bologna, *sfoglini* use a *mattarello* (a narrow, long wooden rolling pin) to roll out *sfoglie* on a *tagliere* (a large wooden board). These are available at different price points online, and are worth getting if you make pasta regularly. But if you don't want to purchase these specific tools, you can certainly use whatever you have (a smooth countertop or table and a regular rolling pin–or even a wine bottle). You can also fashion your own tools (see page 29).

CUTTING AND SHAPING

Have **plastic trash can liners** on hand for covering your *sfoglia* to cure the pasta (see page 35) and to keep it from drying out as you work. I use 3 gal [11 L] black trash can liners, but any **unscented plastic covering** works. You'll need a **very sharp chef's knife** to cut tagliatelle, pappardelle, and *maltagliati*. Use an **accordion pastry cutter** set to the desired width to cut dough into the required quadrilateral shape for filled pastas. To achieve a crimped edge for *strichetti* and *caramelle*, use a **fluted pastry wheel**.

A **large pastry brush**, or even a new paintbrush, is ideal for dusting off your work surface. *Garganelli* call for a *pettina* (pasta comb) for leaving impressions on the dough. It is available online or you can use a sushi mat and a Sharpie™ with the pocket clip broken off to get the same scored result. A clean **spray bottle** filled with water and set to the fine mist setting is ideal for spritzing dough if it feels dry while shaping.

COOKING AND TRANSFERRING PASTA

You will need **small**, **medium**, and **large pots** for preparing these recipes, including a **large heavy-bottomed pot** for meat-based sauces. You will also need **medium** and **large skillets** and **high-sided sauté pans**.

I recommend using **tongs** or **forceps** for handling long pastas and a **spider**, **spork**, or **slotted spoon** for removing filled pastas from boiling water.

For boiling pasta, I love my 8 qt [7.5 L] All-Clad stainless steel pot, but you can use any large pot. In Bologna, I cooked pasta in the thinnest, most warped aluminum pots you've probably ever seen and it was delicious all the same. Just be sure there's plenty of water with respect to the quantity of pasta you are cooking.

PREPPING SAUCES AND FILLINGS

Pass meats and vegetables for ragùs through a **meat grinder** (or meat grinder attachment) **fitted with a medium or large die** (as the recipe instructs). If you don't have one, ask your butcher to grind the meat or chop it with a knife into small pieces. Pulse the vegetables in a food processor until finely chopped.

GRATERS

A **Microplane**™ or **box grater with very small holes** is key for grating Parmigiano-Reggiano and other hard cheeses into a fine, powdery consistency. In that form, it melts faster and more evenly and is less likely to clump.

BENCH SCRAPER

A **bench scraper** is used for Master Dough recipes and is also handy for cleaning your work surface.

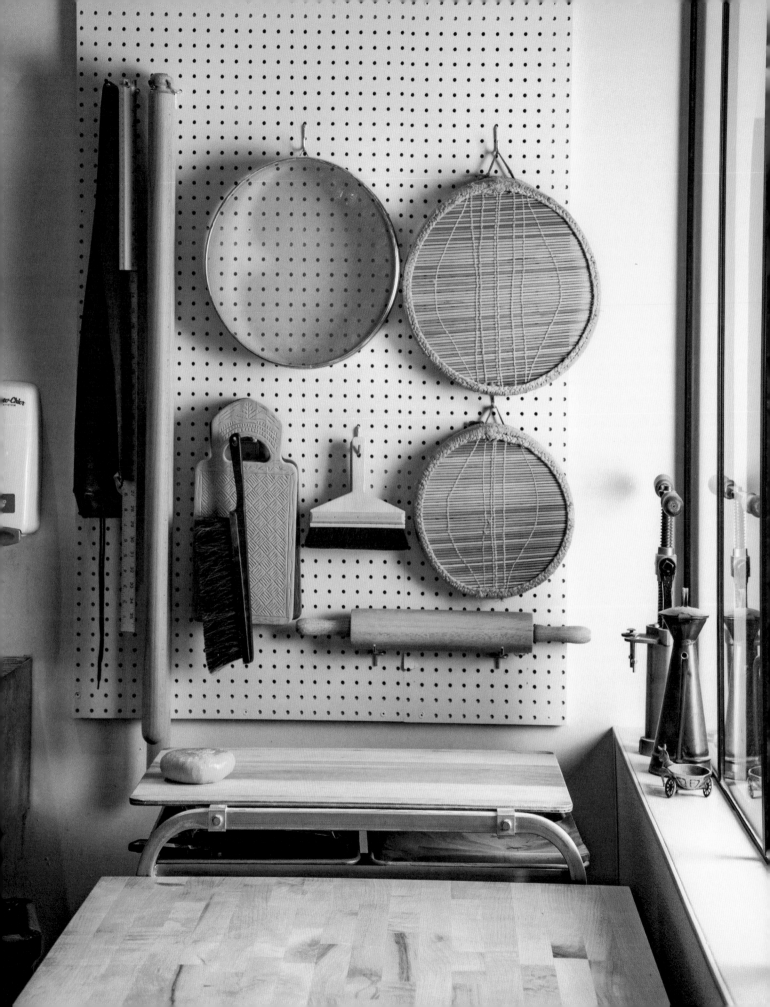

Rolling Tool Hacks

Making your own *tagliere* and *mattarello* requires little more than a trip to your local hardware store and some elbow grease. Even if you do have ready access to store-bought versions, there's surely an extra level of satisfaction making pasta with tools you've also created yourself.

TO MAKE A TAGLIERE

Start by measuring your largest kitchen counter area. To accommodate my recipes, the board needs to be at least 24 in [61 cm] deep and 32 in [81 cm] long. This is a good size in general, too. (Even though the dough is rolled out into a circle, *tagliere* aren't square because you need a little extra horizontal space to turn the rolled out pasta into shapes.) If your counter is smaller than that, plan to use the board on a sturdy desk or table.

Bring these measurements to your hardware store and have them cut a ½ to ¾ in [12 mm to 2 cm] thick untreated, unpressurized wooden board to your specified dimensions. If possible, get Baltic birch plywood because the wood is smooth and compact; pine and maple will work, too. At home, sand the entire board with extra-fine 180-grit sandpaper until very smooth. Finish sanding with 320-grit sandpaper. Remove any dust with a brush or dry cloth. Never wash your *tagliere*.

TO MAKE A MATTARELLO

This is even easier because this is really just a long stick. (These days *mattarelli* are cylindrical; that was hardly a given before the advent of perfectly calibrated rolling pins around 50 years ago.) Buy an untreated, unpressurized solid wooden dowel from the hardware store that is 2 to 2½ in [5 to 6 cm] in diameter and, ideally, as long as the width of your work surface. Generally speaking, 40 in [100 cm] is a good length, although you can get away with one as short as 30 in [76 cm] for the recipe yields in this book. If you can, choose pine because it's affordable and readily available or maple because it's durable.

Sand the dowel all over with extra-fine 180-grit sandpaper until very smooth. Finish sanding with 320-grit sandpaper. Remove any dust with a brush or dry cloth. Never wash your *mattarello*. To preserve it for as long as possible, store it in a long canvas or cotton sheath/bag in a dry place.

INGREDIENTS

SALT

For general cooking, I use kosher salt because it doesn't contain additives.

BLACK PEPPER

Use whole peppercorns and grind them fresh for each use. Commercial ground black pepper is too fine and lacks character.

EGGS

The recipes in this book were developed and tested with extra-large organic eggs. Some of the dough recipes call for eggs by weight rather than a specific number of whole eggs. In those cases, to measure the proper amount, place a small bowl on your digital scale and tare it (to tare means to reset the scale to 0). Knowing that extra large eggs weigh about 60 g [2.15 oz] without their shell, crack the necessary number of eggs into the bowl. (To crack them the bolognese way, strike two together; amazingly, only one will break.) Extract some of the whites until you have the desired weight. Increasing the ratio of yolk to whites makes the mixture fattier and more flavorful. Beat the egg(s) before adding them to the flour. Read more about eggs on page 39.

FLOUR

All four Master Dough recipes call for "00" flour, which is more finely milled than regular flour. This allows it to better absorb liquid and results in a more supple dough. I like Caputo "00" flour, which is available at specialty stores and online. I specifically use the "00" pasta and gnocchi flour in the brown bag. King Arthur makes a good substitute and is available in many supermarkets.

SEMOLINA

One recipe calls for semolina, which is coarsely ground durum wheat. It's also useful for tossing with raw pasta strands or gnocchi to keep them from sticking. (The large grains don't get absorbed by and change the dough the way a more powdery flour would.)

STRUTTO (LARD)

Strutto is rendered pork fat and can be made in a variety of ways, most commonly by heating the fatty parts of the pig and melting them to obtain a soft, spreadable fat. You can purchase it at butcher shops or supermarkets, or make your own by heating pancetta or another fatty pork cut over low heat and draining off and cooling the liquefied fat. *There's no substitute for this ingredient*, which is essential to reproducing the flavors of bolognese cooking. (Leaf lard, made by rendering the soft fat from around a pig's kidneys and loin, is fine to use.)

CANNED TOMATOES

Use whole canned tomatoes rather than crushed. The latter tend to be made with scraps and, as a result, aren't as good. I like Bianco DiNapoli brand, which is available in specialty stores and online, but you can use any quality canned tomato, preferably San Marzano and ideally organic.

PARMIGIANO-REGGIANO

Use authentic Parmigiano-Reggiano and always grate it fresh. (Every cheese bearing the name "Parmigiano-Reggiano" adheres to specific production rules.) Never buy pre-grated cheese, as it is almost always low quality, lacking in flavor, and too dry.

Master Doughs

There are four Master Dough recipes in the book. Three are for pasta sheets—Sfoglia di Acqua e Farina (Flour and Water Dough; page 34), Sfoglia all'Uovo (Egg Dough; page 38), and Sfoglia Verde agli Spinaci (Spinach Dough; page 42). The fourth is for gnocchi—Gnocchi di Ricotta (Ricotta Dumplings; page 46). Gnocchi are not *sfoglia*-based, but are such an integral part of bolognese cuisine I'd be remiss not to include them.

Each pasta dough has different characteristics based on its ingredients, making it suitable for certain shapes and not for others. The chapters that follow these recipes teach you how to make fourteen different types of pasta from the three pasta Master Doughs in addition to the gnocchi. Each shape is then paired with traditional sauces. (For more on pairing shapes and sauces, see page 25.) *Buon lavoro!*

SFOGLIA DI ACQUA E FARINA

FLOUR AND WATER DOUGH

In Bologna—and elsewhere in Italy—Flour and Water Dough is an expression of frugality. Eggs were once a precious ingredient and only the wealthy could enjoy them in their daily pasta. Middle- and working-class people reserved egg-based pasta doughs for holidays, weekends, and special guests.

Water hydrates the flour more efficiently than beaten eggs, therefore you need less of it to have a properly hydrated dough—the hydration is 49 percent versus 57 percent for the egg-based doughs.

MAKES TWO 340 G [ABOUT 12 OZ] PASTA DOUGH BALLS, SERVING 6

454 G [1 LB] "00" FLOUR, PLUS MORE FOR DUSTING

225 G [JUST LESS THAN 8 OZ] TEPID WATER

Make the pasta dough: Sift the flour onto your work surface and make an 8 in [20 cm]–diameter well in the center. You should be able to see the work surface in the middle and the well's walls should be high enough to contain the water.

Pour the water into the well. Working from the interior edge of the well, use a fork to incorporate a bit of the flour with the water. Continue incorporating a bit of flour at a time until the dough is the consistency of pancake batter. Clean off any flour mixture stuck to the fork and add it to the dough.

Using a bench scraper, scrape any remaining flour from the work surface into the dough. Working in a clockwise motion, cut the dough together as though you are making biscuits: scrape, fold, and cut. Continue working the dough until a shaggy mass forms, 2 to 3 minutes. Parts of the mass will be rather wet, while other parts will be floury. Scrape any dough from the bench scraper into the mass.

KNEAD THE PASTA DOUGH: With both hands, pull the far end of the dough toward you quickly and energetically, fold it over itself, then push it away from you using the heels of your palms. Rotate the dough a quarter turn and repeat the kneading for 3 to 5 minutes until the dough is a compact mass. The dough will be slightly tacky.

Using the bench scraper, scrape any dry bits of dough from your work surface and discard. Wash, but do not dry, your hands and continue kneading the dough as before until it is relatively smooth with a cellulite-like texture, an indication of gluten formation, 3 to 5 minutes more.

Wrap the dough tightly, seam-side up, in plastic wrap and smooth out any air pockets. Set aside to rest at room temperature for 15 minutes.

SHAPE THE PASTA DOUGH: Unwrap the dough. Halve it with a sharp knife, cutting in a sawing motion. On a lightly floured surface, knead one piece of dough energetically with both hands, anchoring the dough with your non-dominant hand as you pull the far end of the dough toward you, then press down, through, and away with your dominant hand. Turn the dough counterclockwise using your non-dominant hand, moving it as you knead in 1 to 2 in [2.5 to 5 cm] increments, like the hour markings on a clock.

If the dough feels too dry, spray it and your hands with water, a little at a time, until it loses its dryness. If you are closing the round ball and find the folded end (back door) is not sealing, spray that with a touch of water to help it along. Continue kneading until the dough is soft and smooth all the way around, 3 to 5 minutes. Repeat with the second piece of dough.

Place each dough ball in the middle of its own piece of plastic wrap measuring about 12 in [30.5 cm] square. Working with one ball at a time, pull one corner of the plastic wrap up and lay it over the ball. Then, turning and rotating as you go, make 15 to 20 tiny pleated folds of plastic, almost like a candy wrapper, until the ball is fully and tightly sealed. The plastic wrap will follow the contour of the dough, which will create even pressure and support from all sides and prevent a flat surface or hard edge from developing when wrapping the dough. Set the dough balls aside to rest at room temperature for 2 to 3 hours, or up to 24 hours in the refrigerator, before rolling.

The dough will keep, refrigerated and tightly wrapped in plastic wrap, for up to 2 days. Do not freeze it. You can roll it right away. There's no need to let refrigerated flour and water dough come to room temperature first.

The longer the Flour and Water Dough, Egg Dough (see page 38), and Spinach Dough (see page 42) stay in the refrigerator, the softer and less elastic they become. If your dough is tight—that is, it won't roll out easily, springing back rather than elongating—"relax" it by refrigerating it for up to 24 hours. The longer these doughs rest, inside or outside the refrigerator, the more their extensibility increases and their elasticity decreases.

SHAPING

When shaping dough into a ball before resting, aim for a round and very smooth ball. The rounder and more consistent the ball, the rounder and more consistent the *sfoglia* will be once rolled out.

WRAPPING

Tightly wrapping the pasta dough is essential. Air pockets create humidity, which leaves wet spots on the dough's surface and results in an inconsistent texture.

RESTING

The period between kneading and shaping the dough is called bench rest. This time allows the dough to build more gluten strength, while also aiding the dough's development and texture so it is strong, but not so strong that you can't readily roll it out.

CURING

Before cutting tagliatelle (see page 88), pappardelle (see page 76), and *maltagliati* (see page 100), you will need to cure the *sfoglia*, a process that allows it to dry slowly and gently. Roll a *sfoglia* to the recommended thickness (see page 50), then set it aside on your work surface until it's dry to the touch, but not cracking or cupping on the perimeter, 7 to 10 minutes.

Flip the *sfoglia* and dry the other side.

Next, fold the eastern half of the *sfoglia* so the edge is aligned with the center. Now bring up the western edge and fold it over the central fold to form a long rectangular strip. Fold the southern edge to the center of the strip and fold the northern edge over the central fold, forming a square. Place the folded *sfoglia* on a clean, plastic trash can liner and fold the plastic like an envelope over the *sfoglia* to cover it completely. Set aside for 10 minutes.

The plastic provides a humid atmosphere and lets the *sfoglia* acclimate to a new, lower hydration. Unwrap the *sfoglia* from the plastic and transfer it to a clean work surface. It will feel tighter, but still soft and supple, like cured leather. Unfold the *sfoglia* and let dry for 1 to 2 minutes more before cutting.

SFOGLIA ALL'UOVO

EGG DOUGH

The classic recipe for *sfoglia all'uovo* uses 100 g of flour per large egg. In Bologna, *sfoglini* eyeball these ingredients, making adjustments as needed until they can feel with their fingertips that the dough is perfectly developed, a sign it will roll out into a proper *sfoglia*. What they are really feeling is a dough that is hydrated and has reached the ideal balance of elasticity and extensibility. If a dough has too much elasticity, it will keep bouncing back and be impossible to roll out to the desired diameter—and, by extension, thinness. If, on the other hand, the dough is too extensible (too easy to push and pull), it is overly hydrated and it will be nearly impossible for it to hold its shape once rolled.

Unlike in American restaurant kitchens, in Bologna intense debates about hydration are "not a thing." Bolognesi *feel* the dough and—with lots of practice—you may, too.

But here I think it's essential to provide a more concrete recipe with fewer variables. After years of experimentation, I landed on a recipe that is easy to nail anywhere. It features a precise proportion of egg to flour, which results in a 57 percent hydration dough—hydration level refers to the proportion of liquid to flour—making it especially ideal for filled pasta such as tortellini.

The moisture from the egg hydrates the flour, activating the gluten. Meanwhile, the egg white and yolk provide protein and fat, respectively, lending strength, pliability, and elasticity. I have engineered the dough so all these features are in balance and the resulting pasta has the structure and strength needed for both cut and filled pasta shapes. To that end and as noted in "Measurements" (see page 24), I use metric units ONLY for my Master Dough *sfoglia* recipes. Giving both the flour and egg measurements in grams ensures a better, more consistent result. Using grams also eliminates the variable of using whole eggs, which can vary slightly in weight.

MAKES TWO 355 G [ABOUT 12.5 OZ] PASTA DOUGH BALLS, SERVING 6

454 G [1 LB] "00" FLOUR, PLUS MORE FOR DUSTING

258 G [9.1 OZ] EGGS, BEATEN (SEE EGGS, PAGE 30, FOR MEASURING INFORMATION)

MAKE THE PASTA DOUGH: Sift the flour onto your work surface and make an 8 in [20 cm] diameter well in the center. You should be able to see the work surface in the middle and the well's walls should be high enough to contain the eggs.

Pour the eggs into the well. Working from the interior edge of the well, use a fork to incorporate a bit of the flour with the eggs. Continue incorporating a bit of flour at a time until the dough is the consistency of pancake batter. Clean off any flour mixture stuck to the fork and add it to the dough.

Using a bench scraper, scrape any remaining flour from the work surface into the dough. Working in a clockwise motion, cut the dough together as though you are making biscuits: scrape, fold, and cut (see previous spread). Continue working the dough until a shaggy mass forms, 2 to 3 minutes. Parts of the mass will be rather wet, while other parts will be floury. Scrape any dough from the bench scraper into the mass.

KNEAD THE PASTA DOUGH: With both hands, pull the far end of the dough toward you quickly and energetically, fold it over itself, then push it away from you using the heels of your palms. Rotate the dough a quarter turn and repeat the kneading for 3 to 5 minutes until the dough is a compact mass. The dough will be slightly tacky.

Using the bench scraper, scrape any dry bits of dough from your work surface and discard. Wash, but do not dry, your hands and continue kneading the dough as before until it is relatively smooth with a cellulite-like texture, an indication of gluten formation, 3 to 5 minutes more.

Wrap the dough tightly in plastic wrap, seam-side up, and smooth out any air pockets. Set aside to rest at room temperature for 15 minutes.

SHAPE THE PASTA DOUGH: Unwrap the dough. Halve it with a sharp knife, cutting in a sawing motion. On a lightly floured surface, knead one piece of dough energetically with both hands, anchoring the dough with your non-dominant hand as you pull the far end of the dough toward you, then press down, through, and away, with your dominant hand. Turn the dough counterclockwise using your non-dominant hand, moving it as you knead in 1 to 2 in [2.5 to 5 cm] increments, like the hour markings on a clock.

If the dough feels too dry, spray it and your hands with water, a little at a time, until it loses its dryness. If you are closing the round ball and find the folded end (or back door) is not sealing, spray that with a touch of water to help it along. Continue kneading until the dough is soft and smooth all the way around, 3 to 5 minutes. Repeat with the second piece of dough.

Place each dough ball in the middle of its own piece of plastic wrap measuring about 12 in [30.5 cm] square. Working with one ball at a time, pull one corner of the plastic wrap up and lay it over the ball. Then, turning and rotating as you go, make 15 to 20 tiny pleated folds of plastic, almost like a candy wrapper, until the ball is fully and tightly sealed. The plastic wrap will follow the contour of the dough, which will create even pressure and support from all sides and prevent a flat surface or hard edge from developing when wrapping the dough. Set the dough balls aside to rest at room temperature for 2 to 3 hours or up to 24 hours in the refrigerator before rolling.

The dough will keep, refrigerated and tightly wrapped in plastic wrap, for up to 2 days. Do not freeze it. Before rolling, set the wrapped dough on the counter and let it come to room temperature, about 30 minutes. *This is a must for refrigerated egg doughs.*

EGGS

The first time I broke open an egg at La Vecchia Scuola Bolognese, it was like magic. The yolk was so intensely colorful it practically glowed. It was not at all like the pale yellow orbs typically found in eggs back home in the United States. Thanks to a diet of insects and corn, many chickens in Italy lay eggs with yolks ranging in color from light orange to nearly red. In fact, a synonym in Italian for *tuorlo* (yolk) is *rosso* (red). Orange-red yolks can also be attained by increasing a chicken's beta-carotene consumption, or even feeding it capsicum or marigold petals. The yolk's color influences the pigment of egg-based pasta doughs, although the hues are mellowed by the flour.

Eggs bring a lot more to bolognese pasta than just their tint. Without the fat-rich yolk, there would be no elasticity to the rolled out dough—so strands, such as tagliatelle, would lack character, as would filled pastas, which benefit from a bit of stretch to contain their filling. The protein-rich albumen, on the other hand, imparts strength that gives the pasta its bite when cooked. The egg makes Bologna's most traditional pasta shapes possible. Without this main ingredient, the pages of this book would be mostly blank. No matter where you are, for the best and most beautiful dough, use the highest quality eggs you can find.

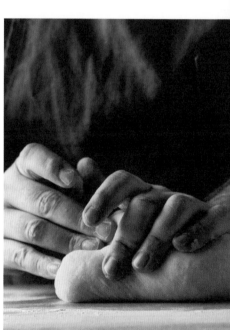

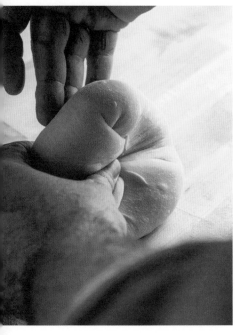

SFOGLIA VERDE AGLI SPINACI

SPINACH DOUGH

Blanched spinach gives this dough, which is used for lasagna (page 64), *balanzoni* (page 160), and *smeraldine* (page 184), its vibrant green color. The first few times I worked with Spinach Dough, I found it very disorienting. I was accustomed to egg dough, which you can see through after rolling it past a certain point to assess how thick it is. When rolling Spinach Dough, take your time and use your sense of touch. Once you get a sense of how it feels when it's the correct thickness, aim for that every time. This knowledge comes with practice.

There's no need here for fancy baby spinach—any type from your local supermarket will do. I even know a few home cooks in Bologna who use the precooked frozen stuff. If you'd like to do the same, defrost it, dry it very well, and substitute 65 g [2¼ oz] for the fresh spinach; no need to blanch it. Either way, process the spinach until very smooth so it doesn't inhibit the dough's gluten development.

MAKES TWO 385 G [ABOUT 13.5 OZ] PASTA DOUGH BALLS, SERVING 6

KOSHER SALT

250 G [8¾ OZ] FRESH SPINACH (SEE HEADNOTE FOR A FROZEN OPTION)

250 G [8¾ OZ] EGGS, BEATEN (SEE EGGS, PAGE 30, FOR MEASURING INFORMATION)

454 G [1 LB] "00" FLOUR

Bring a large pot of water to a boil over high heat. Season the water with salt (see page 25). When the salt dissolves, working in batches to avoid overcrowding, add the spinach. Boil just until the stems soften, 30 to 40 seconds. Using a spider, remove the spinach and spread it on a tray. Let cool for about 20 minutes. Return the water to a boil before adding the next batch. When all the spinach is cooked and cool enough to handle, wrap it in a clean, dry dish towel and squeeze out all the excess water. The spinach must be very dry.

In the bowl of a food processor, combine the spinach and eggs. Process on high speed until smooth and bright green, about 2 minutes.

MAKE THE PASTA DOUGH: Sift the flour onto your work surface and make an 8 in [20 cm] diameter well in the center. You should be able to see the work surface in the middle and the well's walls should be high enough to contain the spinach mixture.

Pour the spinach mixture into the well. Working from the interior edge of the well, use a fork to incorporate a bit of the flour with the mixture. Continue incorporating a bit of flour at a time until the interior edge of the well becomes thin and the dough is thick and has the consistency of pancake batter. Clean off any flour mixture stuck to the fork and add it to the dough.

Using a bench scraper, scrape any flour from the work surface into the dough. Working in a clockwise motion, cut the dough together as though you are making biscuits: scrape, fold, and cut (see pages 36–37). Continue working the dough until a shaggy mass forms, 2 to 3 minutes. Parts of the mass will be rather wet, while other parts will be floury. Scrape any dough from the bench scraper into the mass.

KNEAD THE PASTA DOUGH: With both hands, pull the far end of the dough toward you quickly and energetically, fold it over itself, then push it away from you using the heels of your palms. Rotate the dough a quarter turn and repeat the kneading until the dough is a compact mass, 3 to 5 minutes. The dough will be slightly tacky. Transfer the dough to a clean part of your work surface.

Using the bench scraper, scrape any dry bits of dough from your work surface and discard.

Wash, but do not dry, your hands and continue kneading the dough as before until it is relatively smooth with a cellulite-like texture, an indication of gluten formation, 3 to 5 minutes more.

Wrap the dough tightly, seam-side up, in plastic wrap, smoothing out any air pockets. Set aside to rest at room temperature for 15 minutes.

SHAPE THE PASTA DOUGH: Unwrap the dough. Halve it with a sharp knife, cutting in a sawing motion. On a lightly floured surface, knead one piece of dough energetically with both hands, anchoring the dough with your non-dominant hand as you pull the far end of the dough toward you, then press down, through, and away with your dominant hand. Turn the dough counterclockwise using your non-dominant hand, moving it in 1 to 2 in [2.5 to 5 cm] increments as you knead, like the hours on a clock.

If the dough feels too dry, spray it and your hands with water, a little at a time, until it has lost its dryness. If you are closing the round ball and find the folded end (back door) is not sealing, spray that with a touch of water to help it along. Continue kneading until the dough is soft and smooth all the way around, 3 to 5 minutes. Repeat with the second piece of dough.

Place each dough ball in the middle of its own piece of plastic wrap measuring about 12 in [30.5 cm] square. Working with one ball at a time, pull one corner of the plastic wrap up and lay it over the ball. Then, turning and rotating as you go, make 15 to 20 tiny pleated folds of plastic, almost like a candy wrapper, until it is fully and tightly sealed. The plastic wrap will follow the contour of the dough, which will create even pressure and support from all sides and prevent a flat surface or hard edge from developing when wrapping the dough. Set the dough balls aside to rest at room temperature for 2 to 3 hours, or up to 24 hours in the refrigerator, before rolling.

The dough will keep, refrigerated and tightly wrapped in plastic wrap, for up to 2 days. Do not freeze. Before rolling, set the wrapped dough on the counter and let it come to room temperature, about 30 minutes. *This is a must for refrigerated egg doughs.*

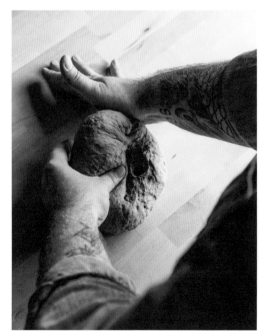

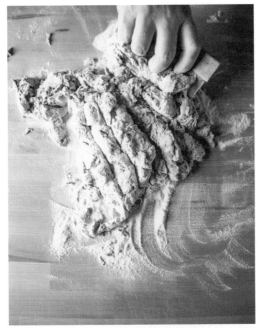

GNOCCHI DI RICOTTA

RICOTTA DUMPLINGS

While gnocchi *di patate*, potato dumplings, may be more widely known outside Italy, ricotta dumplings are a staple in Emilia-Romagna. Both are bite-size and pair well with a variety of sauces, but the ricotta version is much softer than its potato-based cousin.

Gnocchi di Ricotta are made with aerated ricotta, which lends a soft texture to the pasta and makes the gnocchi a flavorful vehicle for sauces. I use cow's milk ricotta to make these because it's the standard in Emilia-Romagna, the cow's milk cheese capital of the universe, but the recipe works well with other types of ricotta, too, and you can absolutely substitute sheep, goat, or even buffalo's milk cheese. As you work the dough, you can tell when it is properly developed if, when you poke it gently, it bounces back ever so slightly. The key is to build just enough gluten to hold it together, resulting in a light and pillowy pasta.

MAKES ABOUT 794 G [28 OZ], SERVING 6

375 G [13¼ OZ] RICOTTA

125 G [4⅖ OZ] EGGS, BEATEN (SEE EGGS, PAGE 30, FOR MEASURING INFORMATION)

½ CUP [50 G] FINELY GRATED PARMIGIANO-REGGIANO

10 G [ABOUT ⅓ OZ] KOSHER SALT

5 GRATES OR 1 PINCH FRESH NUTMEG

234 G [8¼ OZ] "00" FLOUR, PLUS MORE FOR DUSTING

SEMOLINA, FOR DUSTING

Using a bench scraper, press the ricotta through a fine-mesh sieve into a large bowl and set aside. Alternatively, pulse the ricotta in the bowl of a food processor until smooth, about 15 seconds.

Add the eggs, Parmigiano-Reggiano, salt, nutmeg, and one third of the flour to the ricotta. Whisk until smooth, about 1 minute. Pour the remaining flour onto your work surface and spread it evenly into a circle about 10 in [25 cm] in diameter and about ¼ in [6 mm] thick. Add the ricotta mixture to the center.

Using the bench scraper, cut the flour into the ricotta as you would cut butter into biscuits, pushing the tool to the center of the mass, folding, and cutting, incorporating the flour a little bit at a time until you have a very shaggy mass. Parts of the mass will be rather wet, while other parts will be floury.

Using your hands, gently pull the top third of the dough toward you, then gently press down and away from you. Give the dough a half turn and repeat the kneading until the dough is smooth and soft, about 4 minutes. If the dough sticks, lightly dust your work surface with more flour.

Heavily dust a clean work surface twice the diameter of the dough ball with semolina. Place the dough in the center and cover it with a clean bowl or pot roughly twice the size of the ball. Let rest for 45 minutes.

Lightly dust the top of the dough with semolina. Using a *mattarello*, gently and evenly flatten the dough into a square about ½ in [12 mm] thick and 14 in [35.5 cm] in diameter. Lightly dust the dough once more with semolina. Using a pizza cutter, cut the dough closest to you horizontally into a ½ in [12 mm] strip. Repeat once more. Gently roll the strips toward you in the semolina. This will coat them in semolina, preventing sticking and making room for the next strip. Use more semolina, as needed, to prevent sticking. Repeat with the remaining dough, working in pairs of strips.

Cut each strip into ½ in [12 mm] pieces. Once all the strips are cut, gently toss the gnocchi in a handful of semolina and transfer to a parchment paper–lined baking sheet. Refrigerate, uncovered, for at least 1 hour.

If you're not going to use the gnocchi now, arrange them on a parchment paper–lined tray so they don't touch. Tightly wrap the tray in plastic wrap and put the tray in the freezer. Once frozen, transfer the gnocchi to a plastic freezer bag and return to the freezer.

To defrost, spread them on a tray and set aside at room temperature for 10 minutes.

Boil the gnocchi in salted water according to the recipe instructions. Start tasting at 2½ minutes to see if the center is properly cooked. Frozen gnocchi may take a minute or so longer to cook than fresh.

The gnocchi will keep, in the freezer in a plastic freezer bag, for up to 1 month.

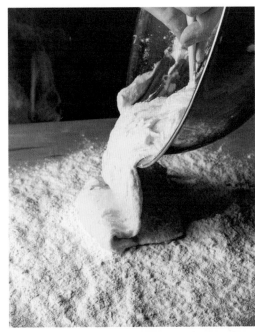
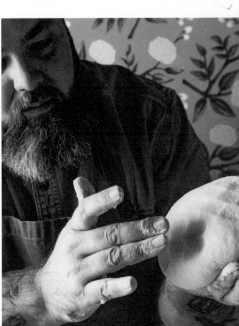

How to Roll a Sfoglia

The goal when rolling out *sfoglia* is to end up with a round sheet thin enough that you can read a newspaper through it. This may sound challenging, but if you start with a properly made dough and carefully follow the steps, you will end up with a respectable *sfoglia*. And like anything else, with practice, the process gets easier and the results better.

There are also different degrees of thickness depending on the shape you are making. For instance, pappardelle is about twice as thick as tagliatelle. To help you visualize and measure the proper thickness for each type of pasta shape in the book, I've broken them down in terms of stacked Post-it® Notes. Use the following guidelines when rolling out *sfoglia*:

- **A thickness of approximately 4 Post-it® Notes:** tagliatelle, *garganelli*, and tortellini

- **A thickness of approximately 7 Post-it® Notes:** *strozzapreti, strichetti, caramelle,* and *cestini*

- **A thickness of approximately 9 Post-it® Notes:** lasagna, pappardelle, *maltagliati, triangoli, tortelloni,* and *balanzoni*

Begin by lightly dusting your work surface with "OO" flour. (Reminder: be sure the surface measures at least 24 in [61 cm] deep and 32 in [81 cm] long to accommodate the rolled out dough.) To do this, take a very small handful of flour, bunch it up in your fist, and throw it against the work surface in a flurry. It will poof up and explode like a cloud of baby powder, and settle down and dust the surface evenly.

Use the same method when dusting pasta dough. When working with the dough or a rolled-out *sfoglia*, use flour sparingly. Flour will expedite the drying process and make the *sfoglia* harder to work with.

Place the dough on the lightly floured work surface and gently flatten the dough ball with the soft part of your palm to form a uniform disk with a thickness about 6 in [15 cm] wide (Fig 1–2).

Once your dough is flattened, position the *mattarello* at 9 and 3 o'clock and, with firm, even pressure, roll it forward, creating the top half of an oval. Bring the pin back to the center and roll back toward you, ending with an egg-shaped disk (Fig 3). Rotate the *sfoglia* 90 degrees and roll forward from the center again. Bring the pin back to the center, and with firm, even pressure, roll back toward you, forming a round disk (Fig 4–5).

When the *sfoglia* is small, use larger movements and apply even pressure with the *mattarello*, rolling forward from the center of the dough, then rotating the *sfoglia* a quarter turn with your hand. Repeat until the *sfoglia* measures about 14 in [45 cm] in diameter (Fig 6–10).

Now that you have a larger *sfoglia*, you can begin to allow the bottom fifth of it to hang off the table, toward you. This way, as the *sfoglia* continues to grow, you won't overextend yourself trying to roll the top of the sheet. It also creates an anchor for the *sfoglia* to stretch, letting it stretch more easily, as if the entire *sfoglia* was on the table without sliding away.

To move the *sfoglia*, use the *mattarello*. Place the *mattarello* about 5 in [12 cm] from the top edge of the *sfoglia* and gently fold this portion toward you over the *mattarello* (Fig 13 and 24).

Using both thumbs, cinch the sheet tightly on the *mattarello*, holding it in place but not pinching (Fig 14 and 25), Tuck the top edge of the *sfoglia* in place, holding it with your thumb, and roll the *sfoglia* onto the *mattarello* toward you like a map rolled on a spool (Fig 15 and 26).

Give the dough a quarter turn and unfurl it flat (Fig 16 and 27). As you unfurl it, lay it flat, making sure there is no air between the *sfoglia* and the table. To de-gas (this pushes any trapped air out from underneath), gently roll the *mattarello* over the *sfoglia*, applying no pressure whatsoever, and then roll it back to the center (Fig 17).

Now, use the rolling method described in "Mastering the Mattarello" (see sidebar). Position your hands wide on the *mattarello* and guide your hands along the perimeter of the pasta, pushing toward 12 o'clock, creating a round (Fig 23). You can start working the top quarter of the clock as needed: 10, 11, 12, 1, and 2 o'clock (Fig 32–33). Roll forward with even pressure and guide it back with cupped fingers. You will roll each hour of the clock four to six times, resulting in 20 to 30 rolls for this quarter of the clock. Add additional flour only if the dough is sticking to the *mattarello* or the table.

Once have finished your 20 to 30 rolls, use your *mattarello* to turn the dough and continue the process until you reach the desired thinness for the shape you are making (see facing page).

Think of your dough like a clock on which you only ever work the hours between 10 and 2 o'clock—the top quarter of your *sfoglia*.

MASTERING THE MATTARELLO

Position your hands near the ends of the *mattarello* and loosely grip it as if your hands are the wheel well of a car and the *mattarello* is the wheel.

As you roll, your hands should always follow the perimeter of the dough. Your palms start wide when the *mattarello* is at the widest diameter of the dough and they close in as you reach the 12 o'clock position. Remember to always roll the *mattarello* away from you, pushing with your palms and guiding back with your fingers. And always push the *mattarello* in a forward motion—never in a downward motion. Also, take care not to roll your *mattarello* beyond the dough itself, which results in a pinched edge. Remember the uniformity of thickness is far more important than a perfectly round shape. Once you cut it, nobody will know how round it was, but they will know how uniformly thick it is—or isn't!

1

2

3

6

7

4

5

8

9

10

11

12

13

17

18

19

14

15

16

20

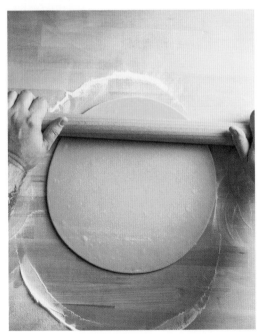

21

22

23

24

25

29

30

31

26

27

28

32

33

34

Troubleshooting

Pasta making is just as much about following a recipe and procedure as it is about trusting your instincts, making small adjustments, and getting to know the dough so intimately you can infer whether it's all coming together—or not—before you even finish kneading. Here are some common issues you may encounter during the process and how to solve them.

MY DOUGH IS DRY AND HARD TO ROLL.

Sprinkle with and knead in water, 1 Tbsp at a time, to loosen it up. Allow the dough to rest overnight, wrapped in plastic, then try rolling again.

MY DOUGH IS TOO WET AND IT'S HARD TO WORK WITH.

If you know you measured the ingredients properly, you may have left the dough uncovered in an environment that is too humid, or your flour is very fresh and still retains a lot of humidity. Sprinkle with and knead in flour, 1 Tbsp at a time, to help the dough come together.

MY SFOGLIA IS STICKING TO THE MATTARELLO AND/OR WORK SURFACE.

Only add flour if the *sfoglia* is really sticking and always show restraint. Too much flour will dry out the dough and cause it to crack around the edges. If the dough is only sticking to the mattarello, dust the *sfoglia* itself with the same kind of flour you used to make the dough.

If the *sfoglia* is sticking to the work surface, dust that. If you're in the rolling phase, use the same kind of flour you used to make the dough. If you're in the cutting or shaping phase, use semolina, which has large grains that won't affect the dough, but will keep it from sticking. Also, the thinner the *sfoglia* gets, the less flour you should use. It's more difficult to shape the drier the *sfoglia* is.

I'M TRYING TO SLICE THE ROLLED OUT SFOGLIA INTO STRANDS, BUT I END UP KIND OF MASHING IT.

Try a sharper knife. Push the knife forward as you cut. You want precise, definitive cuts so each strand is of identical thickness.

MY PASTA TASTES RAW AFTER THE RECOMMENDED COOKING TIME.

You may have rolled the *sfoglia* a little too thick. Keep cooking. The thickness of the pasta determines the length of cooking time. Always double check the thickness before cutting the dough. Taste the pasta constantly as it cooks, and cook until it has lost its raw bite and is tender.

MY PASTA LACKS TEXTURE.

It may be overcooked. Check for doneness earlier next time. And generally taste pasta for doneness constantly as it cooks.

MY FILLED PASTA BROKE OPEN.

Be sure to adequately moisten the entire dough edge before enclosing the filling and then press the edges together (don't miss any spots) with firm pressure. This should seal in the filling tightly. If instead the *sfoglia* cracks or seems too dry to close properly, spritz it all over with a fine mist before shaping the pasta. If you are cooking the pasta in batches and the breaks occur during the first batch, double-check the remaining pieces for any gaps between the edges before cooking them.

MY CESTINI, CARAMELLE, ETC. LOOK REALLY WEIRD.

Don't worry! Everyone's pasta looks like shit when they are first starting out. I know mine did! Just practice and I promise you WILL get better.

PART 2:
PASTA SHAPES & DISHES

LASAGNA ALLA BO[

There are as many lasagna recipes as there are cooks in Italy, yet, with so much variation, there is one regional tradition that stands out among all the others: Bologna's lasagna. It is the lasagna that all others aspire (and fail) to be. This particular incarnation of Italy's famous recipe features sheets of spinach pasta layered with meat ragù and béchamel. My version is straight out of Maestra Alessandra's playbook and it's a dish that graces her table—and mine—every time she invites an honored guest for Sunday lunch.

I feel particularly protective of this recipe and it really bonds me to the maestra. In all the time Alessandra has had La Vecchia Scuola, she never let any student build her lasagna. The dish is so sacred to her that even her daughter wasn't allowed to touch it. One day, about three months into my tenure there, she nonchalantly asked me to roll out a *sfoglia verde*, then brought ragù, béchamel, and a pan over to my counter and said, "*fai*"—make it. It was one of the proudest days of my professional life.

Making lasagna requires several components, so be sure each is ready before you start the assembly. You'll need a pot at least 16 in [40 cm] wide for blanching the pasta sheets. You can also halve the sheets crosswise and use a smaller pot at least 8 in [20 cm] wide.

VERDE
BOLOGNESE

LASAGNE VERDE ALLA BOLOGNESE

MAKES ONE 15 BY 9.5 IN [38 BY 24 CM]
LASAGNA, SERVING 6

UNSALTED BUTTER, FOR GREASING

1 RECIPE SFOGLIA VERDE AGLI SPINACI
(PAGE 42), AT ROOM TEMPERATURE

"00" FLOUR, FOR DUSTING

KOSHER SALT

½ RECIPE RAGÙ DELLA VECCHIA SCUOLA
(PAGE 90)

1 RECIPE BESCIAMELLA (PAGE 70)

6 CUPS [600 G] FINELY GRATED PARMIGIANO-
REGGIANO, PLUS MORE FOR SPRINKLING

Preheat the oven to 375°F [190°C]. Lightly grease a 15 by 9.5 in [38 by 24 cm] baking dish with unsalted butter.

Roll one dough ball to a thickness of 9 Post-it® Notes on a lightly floured surface (see page 50). Using a sharp knife, cut the *sfoglia* into 3 pieces measuring about 16 by 8 in [40 by 20 cm]. Lightly flour another surface and set the pieces on it to dry, uncovered, for about 15 minutes, flipping midway through the drying time. Reserve the scraps, which you may need to fill in any gaps when assembling the lasagna.

Meanwhile, repeat the process with the remaining dough ball.

Line two baking sheets with parchment paper and set aside. Bring a large pot of water to a boil over high heat. Season the water with salt (see page 25). When the salt dissolves, add 1 pasta sheet and blanch for 30 seconds. Using a spider, transfer the pasta to the prepared baking sheet to cool. Once the pasta is cool enough to handle, smooth it out. Repeat with the remaining 5 pasta sheets.

Spread about 1 cup [225 g] of ragù in the prepared baking dish, distributing it evenly. Spread ½ cup [112.5 g] of the *besciamella* over the ragù, distributing it evenly. Place one blanched pasta sheet over the sauce and *besciamella* layer. Spread about 1 cup [225 g] of ragù over the blanched pasta, distributing it evenly, followed by ½ cup [112.5 g] of the *besciamella*, distributing it evenly. Dust with about 1 cup [100 g] of Parmigiano-Reggiano. Continue to layer the pasta with the remaining ragù, *besciamella*, and Parmigiano-Reggiano, ending with the Parmigiano-Reggiano.

Cover the baking dish with aluminum foil and bake for 30 minutes. Remove the foil and bake until the pasta is cooked through and the edges are crispy and browned, about 30 minutes more. Let the lasagna rest for 10 to 15 minutes to firm up before serving. Serve immediately with more Parmigiano-Reggiano on the side.

The cooked lasagna will keep, refrigerated and tightly covered, for up to 5 days or frozen for up to 3 months.

BESCIAMELLA

BÉCHAMEL

**BOLOGNA'S GLORIOUS
HARDWARE STORES**

I'm obsessed with hardware stores in general, and I never miss an opportunity to pop into one of Bologna's many family-owned *ferramente*. Where else can you get keys cut while shopping for otherworldly bronze cherub doorknockers and everyday kitchen equipment? My go-to shop in Bologna is Antica Aguzzeria del Cavallo on Via Drapperie, a street running through the heart of the city that is absolutely packed with food shops.

Since opening their store in 1783, the Bernagozzi family has amassed a vast collection of essential and esoteric items for the home. Not surprisingly, you can usually find me in the pasta-related section. I've spent many happy hours there perusing everything from an array of accordion cutters to bronze pasta tools from the 1960s and '70s that would fetch a pretty penny on eBay, but are very affordable at Antica Aguzzeria del Cavallo (and they don't do mail order). The items are stocked floor to ceiling, so be sure to check your claustrophobia at the door. I guarantee you'll find whatever you need, as well as items you didn't even know existed—or that you needed!

Made with butter, flour, and milk, béchamel is a classic white sauce that's a staple in Italian and French cooking. Bologna's lasagna wouldn't be the same without it. To prevent the sauce from congealing, which would make it difficult to spread between the layers, prepare it last and time its completion to coincide with boiling the pasta sheets. You can also make it ahead and reheat it.

MAKES ABOUT 5 CUPS [1.1 KG]

8 TBSP [1 STICK, OR 112 G] UNSALTED BUTTER

1 CUP [125 G] "00" FLOUR

1 QT [960 ML] WHOLE MILK

1 TSP KOSHER SALT

5 SMALL PINCHES OF GROUND NUTMEG, PREFERABLY FRESHLY GRATED

In a medium sauté pan or skillet over medium heat, melt the butter until frothy and golden. Whisking vigorously, slowly "rain in" the flour. Once all the flour is added, whisk continuously for 3 minutes more. The mixture should appear crumbly, but smell sweet and toasted.

Still whisking continuously, add the milk in a steady stream, whisking until the mixture is very smooth. Season with the salt and nutmeg and whisk to combine. Increase the heat to medium-high and cook the mixture until it is thick enough to coat the back of a wooden spoon, about 2½ minutes. Use now or refrigerate.

The béchamel will keep, refrigerated in an airtight container with plastic wrap laid over the surface, for up to 5 days. To reheat, transfer to a medium sauté pan or skillet and add warm water, as needed, whisking constantly to avoid clumping as the béchamel warms.

PAPPAR

Maestra Alessandra is always quick to remind me that pappardelle are from Tuscany, waving her hand in the general southwestern direction of the Tuscan border whenever they come up. Indeed, the root of pappardelle—*pappare*—comes from the Tuscan dialect and means to eat with gusto. Owing to that region's close proximity to Emilia-Romagna, not to mention the similar method of production, it's not surprising this "foreign" shape is now made in Bologna and considered the cousin of tagliatelle.

While tagiatelle's natural sauce pairing is bolognese meat ragù such as Ragù della Vecchia Scuola (page 90), pappardelle are best dressed with robust sauces and ragùs, owing to the thickness of the noodles.

DELLE

PAPPARDELLE

MAKES ABOUT 710 G [25 OZ], SERVING 6

**1 RECIPE SFOGLIA ALL'UOVO (PAGE 38),
AT ROOM TEMPERATURE**

"00" FLOUR, FOR DUSTING

Roll one dough ball to a thickness of 9 Post-it® Notes on a lightly floured work surface (see page 50). Cure the *sfoglia* (see page 35). Fold the *sfoglia* in half, press gently along the crease, and unfold. Using a sharp knife, cut the *sfoglia* along the crease. Position the half-moon–shaped pieces of *sfoglia* with the round ends closest to you and the cut ends facing away from you. Starting at the round edge of one *sfoglia* crescent, fold the pasta 3 in [7.5 cm] over and continue to fold until you have a loose roll. Repeat with the second crescent.

Beginning at the end of one roll, using a sharp knife, square off the edge and add these irregular pieces to your *maltagliati* pile (see page 100). Continue cutting the *sfoglia* crosswise into 1 in [2.5 cm] thick strips, adding the irregular rounded pieces from the other end of the roll to your *maltagliati* pile. Repeat with the remaining crescent.

Take the pasta strand from the center of one roll, unfurl, and place it on the work surface in a horizontal orientation. Working from the center outward, take the next pasta strand, unfurl, and lay it on the work surface in a horizontal orientation. Repeat with 2 more strands to create a total of 4 stacks. Move the remaining strips together.

Take the pasta strand from the center of the second roll, unfurl, and place it on the work surface in a horizontal orientation. Working from the center outward, take the next pasta strand, unfurl, and lay it on the work surface in a horizontal orientation. Repeat with 2 more strands. Move the remaining cut rolled pasta together. Working from the center outward, repeat the unfurling and stacking process until no rolled pasta remains.

Using one hand, grasp the center of the first stack and let the strands hang. Fold the stack in half and transfer it to a clean work surface, cut-side up. Repeat with the remaining stacks. Use now or refrigerate, in a high-sided container lined with paper towels and loosely covered, for up to 24 hours.

Meanwhile, repeat the process with the remaining dough ball.

To cook, unfurl the pasta rolls onto a tray before dropping them into salted boiling water (see page 25).

PAPPARDELLE AL RAGÙ DI CINGHIALE

PAPPARDELLE WITH WILD BOAR RAGÙ

Wild boars roam the forests of Emilia-Romagna, emerging occasionally to terrorize farm animals and dig up costly vineyard roots. The silver lining of this nuisance is boar-hunting season, which begins in fall. All autumn long, wild boar recipes, especially those featuring long braises and hearty sauces, appear on menus all over Italy. Boar dishes aren't nearly as common in America, although you can buy wild boar meat from gourmet food purveyors and online (it's usually frozen). As it generally lacks the intense gaminess of its Italian counterpart, I compensate for this flavor deficit by using a robust herb bouquet. If you don't have a meat grinder, ask your butcher to grind it for you. Pork shoulder can be substituted for the boar.

SERVES 6; MAKES 4 QT/16 CUPS [3.2 KG] SAUCE

3 LB [1.4 KG] WILD BOAR SHOULDER, OR PORK SHOULDER

5 OZ [140 G] PANCETTA

4 CELERY STALKS, ROUGHLY CHOPPED

1 LARGE YELLOW ONION, ROUGHLY CHOPPED

1 CARROT, ROUGHLY CHOPPED

1 SMALL FENNEL BULB, OUTER LAYER DISCARDED, ROUGHLY CHOPPED

5 OZ [140 G] STRUTTO

6 TO 8 FRESH SAGE LEAVES, TORN

5 JUNIPER BERRIES

2 GARLIC CLOVES, MINCED

1 SPRIG ROSEMARY, PICKED AND CHOPPED

1 BAY LEAF, PREFERABLY FRESH

KOSHER SALT

FRESHLY GROUND BLACK PEPPER

1½ CUPS [360 ML] DRY RED WINE (I LIKE SANGIOVESE)

3 CUPS [675 G] PASSATA DI POMODORO (PAGE 236)

2 CUPS [480 ML] BRODO DI CARNE (PAGE 237), OR LOW-SODIUM CHICKEN BROTH

2 TBSP UNSALTED BUTTER

1 RECIPE PAPPARDELLE (PAGE 76)

½ CUP [50 G] FINELY GRATED PARMIGIANO-REGGIANO

Using a meat grinder, or a grinder attachment, fitted with a large die, grind the boar shoulder into a large bowl (see tip). Set aside. Without cleaning the grinder, grind the pancetta into a small bowl and set aside. Pass the celery, onions, carrots, and fennel through the grinder into a medium bowl and set aside.

In a large heavy-bottomed pot over medium-high heat, melt the *strutto*. Add the ground pancetta. Cook until the fat has rendered, about 4 minutes. Add the sage, juniper berries, garlic, rosemary, and bay leaf. Cook until fragrant, about 30 seconds. Add the ground vegetables. Cook, stirring frequently, until golden brown and softened, about 15 minutes.

Add the ground boar and generously season with salt and a small amount of pepper. Using a wooden spoon, gently mix the meat and vegetables, stirring from the bottom of the pot. Cook until the meat releases its juices, 6 to 8 minutes. Stir in the wine. Cook until the contents of the pan begin to steam. Stir in the *passata* and *brodo*, turn the heat to low, and cook, stirring occasionally, until the meat is fork-tender, 3 to 5 hours. Begin tasting for tenderness and seasoning after 3 hours.

Transfer 5 cups [1.1 kg] of the sauce to a large pot over medium heat. (Store the extra sauce according to the instructions following.) Bring the sauce to a rapid simmer and cook until the sauce reduces slightly, about 3 to 4 minutes. Add the butter and swirl to emulsify. Set the sauce aside.

Bring a large pot of water to a rolling boil over high heat. Season the water with salt (see page 25). When the salt dissolves, unfurl the pappardelle rolls onto a tray. Gather the strands and, working quickly in batches, drop them into the boiling water. Stir to separate the strands and cook until tender, 1 to 2 minutes.

Meanwhile, return the sauce to medium heat. Using tongs, transfer the pasta to the sauce and toss to coat. Add some pasta cooking water, as needed, to loosen the sauce. Serve immediately with the Parmigiano-Reggiano sprinkled on top.

The sauce will keep, refrigerated in an airtight container, for up to 5 days, or frozen for up to 6 months.

I recommend grinding the boar, pancetta, and vegetables using a meat grinder or the accompanying grinder attachment for your stand mixer. If you don't have either, simply cut the boar into 1 in [2.5 cm] cubes and dice the pancetta into ¼ in [6 mm] batons. Boar is rarely available from butcher shops or supermarket meat counters, so you won't be able to rely on your butcher to grind it for you. Pulse the vegetables in the bowl of a food processor.

PAPPARDELLE CON RAGÙ DI ANATRA

PAPPARDELLE WITH DUCK RAGÙ

An earthy sauce of duck dates back to the Renaissance, a time when Bologna was at its peak and diners the city over ate intricate dishes with deeply layered flavors.

SERVES 6

4 DUCK LEGS (32 OZ [908 G]), RINSED AND PATTED DRY

2 OZ [57 G] CHICKEN HEARTS, RINSED AND PATTED DRY

2 OZ [57 G] CHICKEN GIZZARDS, RINSED AND PATTED DRY

KOSHER SALT

FRESHLY GROUND BLACK PEPPER

5 TBSP [70 G] UNSALTED BUTTER

2 OZ [57 G] PROSCIUTTO DI PARMA (SEE PAGE 250), FINELY CHOPPED

5 FRESH SAGE LEAVES

ONE 6 IN [15 CM] SPRIG FRESH ROSEMARY, LEAVES PICKED AND FINELY CHOPPED

2 CELERY STALKS, GROUND OR FINELY CHOPPED

1 LARGE CARROT, FINELY CHOPPED

1 MEDIUM YELLOW ONION, FINELY CHOPPED

1 TBSP TOMATO PASTE

2 CUPS [480 ML] DRY RED WINE

2 CUPS [480 ML] LOW-SODIUM CHICKEN BROTH

1 RECIPE PAPPARDELLE (PAGE 76)

½ CUP [50 G] FINELY GRATED PARMIGIANO-REGGIANO

Season the duck legs, chicken hearts, and chicken gizzards all over with salt and pepper and set aside on a platter.

In a large high-sided sauté pan or skillet over medium heat, melt the butter until frothy and golden. Add the duck legs and cook on both sides until the fat is rendered and the meat is golden, about 15 minutes total. Remove from the pan.

Add the chicken hearts and gizzards to the sauté pan and sear on both sides until golden, about 4 minutes total. Remove from the pan and let cool for about 10 minutes. Pass the hearts and gizzards through a meat grinder, or roughly chop them.

Decrease the heat under the pan to low and add the prosciutto, sage, and rosemary. Cook until the prosciutto is lightly browned, 3 to 4 minutes. Add the celery, carrot, and onion and cook until golden brown and softened, about 15 minutes, stirring occasionally. Add the ground hearts and gizzards and cook for about 4 minutes until browned. Add the tomato paste and stir vigorously to incorporate, 3 to 4 minutes. Stir in the wine, scraping up any browned bits stuck to the bottom of the pan, and cook until the liquid is reduced by half, about 4 minutes. Add the chicken broth. Increase the heat to medium and bring the mixture to a simmer.

Decrease the heat to low and add the duck legs. Half-cover the pan and cook until very tender, about 2 hours.

Remove the duck legs from the sauce and set aside to cool. Increase the heat to medium-high and bring the sauce to a rapid simmer. Cook until thickened, 10 to 15 minutes.

Meanwhile, pull the cooled duck meat from the bones and shred it, discarding any soft skin. Return the meat to the pan. Season to taste with salt and black pepper and set the sauce aside.

Bring a large pot of water to a rolling boil over high heat. Season the water with salt (see page 25). When the salt dissolves, unfurl the pappardelle rolls onto a tray. Gather the strands and, working quickly in batches, drop them into the boiling water. Stir to separate the strands and cook until tender, 1 to 2 minutes.

Meanwhile, return the sauce to medium heat. Using tongs, transfer the pasta to the sauce and toss to coat. Add some pasta cooking water, as needed, to loosen the sauce. Serve immediately with Parmigiano-Reggiano sprinkled on top.

The sauce will keep, refrigerated in an airtight container for up to 4 days or in the freezer for up to 6 months.

PAPPARDELLE ALLA CONTADINA

PAPPARDELLE WITH VEGETABLES

Contadina means "female farmer," and these hard-working women are the keepers of both heirloom produce varieties and disappearing rural traditions. This sauce is a celebration of summer—a pairing of seasonal vegetables cooked in stages to build layers of flavor. You can and should be flexible with the ingredients: in summer, use tomatoes, peppers, and squash, while in winter, adapt with whatever vegetables are available in your market. The only rules of thumb are to select the finest local produce and cook it in stages, beginning with the densest.

SERVES 6

¼ CUP [60 ML] EXTRA-VIRGIN OLIVE OIL

9 OZ [255 G] PANCETTA, CUT INTO ¼ IN [6 MM] BATONS

2 GARLIC CLOVES, SMASHED

1 HEAPING TBSP FRESH MARJORAM LEAVES

½ CUP [20 G] FRESH FLAT-LEAF PARSLEY

3 CELERY STALKS, FINELY DICED

1 LARGE CARROT, FINELY DICED

1 LARGE YELLOW ONION, FINELY DICED

1 LARGE FENNEL BULB, OUTER LAYER DISCARDED, FINELY DICED

KOSHER SALT

FRESHLY GROUND BLACK PEPPER

1 CUP [240 G] DRY WHITE WINE

1 LB [454 G] LUNCHBOX OR BELL PEPPERS, ANY COLOR OR A MIX, THICKLY SLICED

2 LB [908 G] BABY ARTICHOKES, TRIMMED AND QUARTERED

2 LB [908 G] RIPE TOMATOES, DICED

1 LB [454 G] ZUCCHINI, DICED

8 OZ [227 G] EGGPLANT, DICED

2 CUPS [450 G] PASSATA DI POMODORO (PAGE 236)

1 RECIPE PAPPARDELLE (PAGE 76)

1 CUP [100 G] FINELY GRATED PARMIGIANO-REGGIANO

In a large heavy-bottomed pot over medium-high heat, heat the oil until it begins to shimmer. Add the pancetta and cook until crispy and golden and the fat has rendered, 2 to 3 minutes. Add the garlic and cook just until fragrant, about 15 seconds. Add the marjoram and parsley and cook until fragrant, about 30 seconds. Add the celery, carrot, onion, and fennel, season with salt and pepper, and cook until golden brown and softened, about 15 minutes.

Add the wine and cook until it evaporates, about 2 minutes. Add the peppers and artichokes, season with salt and pepper, and cook, stirring frequently, until softened, about 10 minutes. Add the tomatoes, zucchini, and eggplant, season with salt and pepper, and cook, stirring frequently, until the sauce comes together, about 5 minutes more. Stir in the *passata* and cook until the artichokes are tender, about 15 minutes.

Season with salt. Set the sauce aside.

Bring a large pot of water to a rolling boil over high heat. Season the water with salt (see page 25). When the salt dissolves, unfurl the papperdelle rolls onto a tray. Gather the strands and, working quickly in batches, drop them into the boiling water. Stir to separate the strands and cook until tender, 1 to 2 minutes.

Meanwhile, return the sauce to medium heat. Using tongs, transfer the pasta to the sauce and toss to coat. Add some pasta cooking water, as needed, to loosen the sauce. Serve immediately with the Parmigiano-Reggiano sprinkled on top.

The sauce will keep, refrigerated in an airtight container, for up to 7 days.

Lambrusco's Renaissance

Before the 1960s Lambrusco was an obscure regional wine enjoyed alongside Emilia-Romagna's rich cuisine. Not only did it complement the food, its effervescence and tannin served as palate cleansers that would prepare diners for their next bite of prosciutto, mortadella, *lardo*-smeared bruschetta, and other unctuous delicacies. I envy people who knew Lambrusco before its mass production and loss of identity—and quite nearly its soul. Fortunately, in recent years, that situation has been improving.

Lambrusco is, by definition, a sparkling wine made from a family of red grapes of the same name. Depending on the variety, Lambrusco might be blended with other native grapes, such as Malbo Gentile or Ancellotta, which are chosen to balance flavor, structure, or acidity, or to add color. The methods of making Lambrusco transitioned from artisanal to industrial in the 1970s with the arrival of the Charmat Method, which involves fermenting wine in large stainless steel autoclaves, trapping carbon dioxide in the liquid as yeast digests the sugar in the grape juice. The result is a very consistent, though characterless, wine manufactured to feed a global thirst for sweet wines. In fact, most Lambrusco falls under a category called *amabile* (sweet) and is cloying and, frankly, undrinkable.

Over the past several decades, though, small producers, including Camillo Donati, Vittorio Graziano, and Luciano and Sara Saetti, have been returning to the old-school methods of making Lambrusco in the bottle, a process called *metodo ancestrale*. The partially fermented wine is bottled so carbon dioxide is trapped inside the glass bottle as the wine continues to ferment. The result is pleasantly effervescent, complex, and a fitting foil to the luscious foods of Emilia-Romagna.

I like to pair artisanal Lambrusco with Tagliatelle con Ragù della Vecchia Scuola (page 90), Lasagna Verde alla Bolognese (page 68), or any pasta served with a hearty meat ragù, so I'm happy it is becoming more widely available outside Italy. The producers have mentioned exporting to the States, so be sure to ask your local wine shop to stock some bottles if they don't already. And if they can't snag something from those producers, look for Lambrusco made in the *metodo ancestrale*. My favorite Lambrusco vendors in the U.S. are Domaine L.A. in Los Angeles and Discovery Wine in New York City.

TAGLIAT

Tagliatelle's long, thin strands rank beside tortellini as Bologna's most important pasta shape. In both cases the dough is rolled as thinly as possible—seasoned *sfoglini* can roll the dough to a thinness of two Post-it® Notes; you should try for four.

Tagliatelle's most famous pairing is with bolognese meat ragù such as the *maestra*'s Ragù della Vecchia Scuola (page 90). Lest you think the reverence for tagliatelle is mere hyperbole, consider that the city of Bologna has a single tagliatella *dipped in gold*, which they keep in a closed box in Bologna's Chamber of Commerce as a standard against which all strands can be judged.

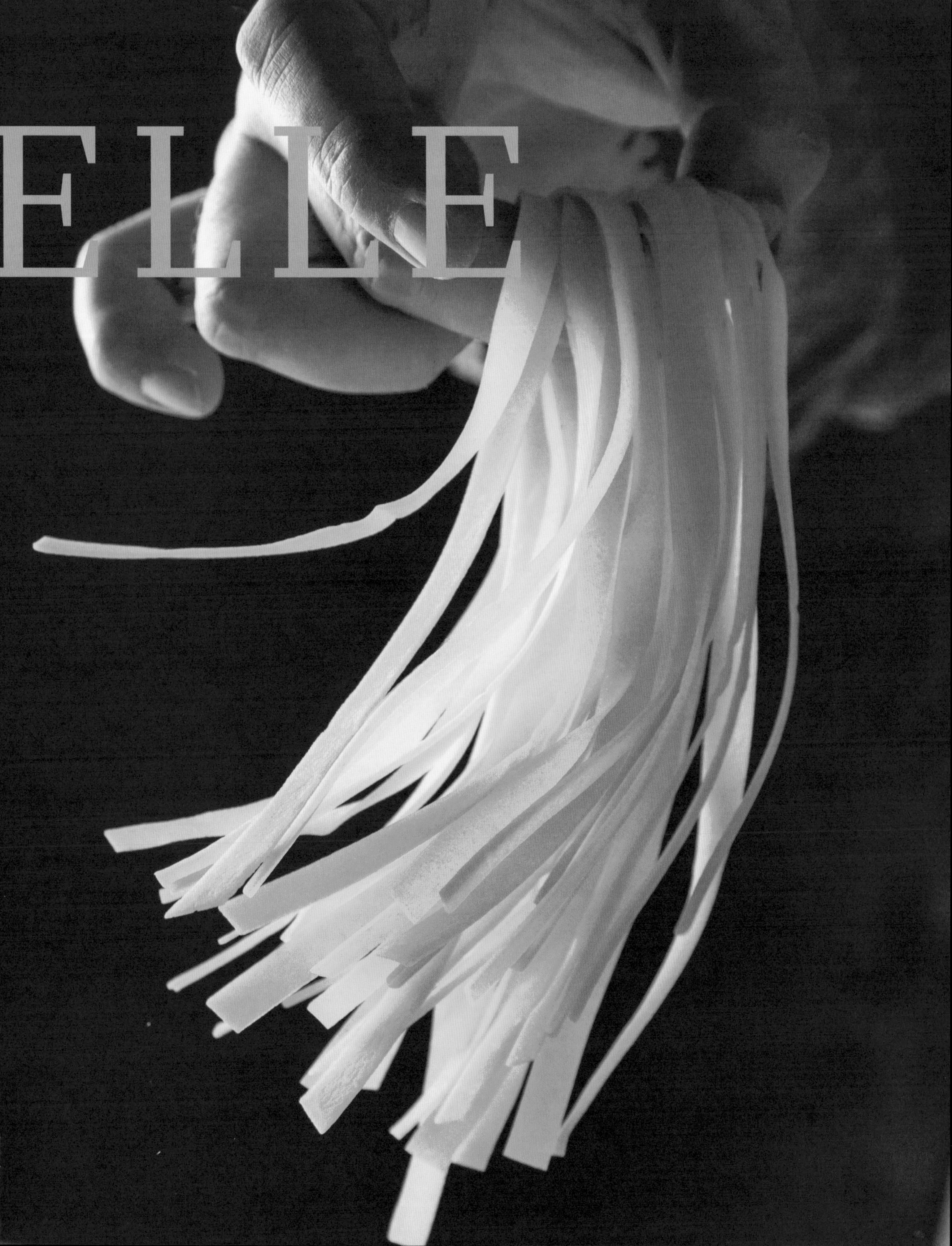
ELLE

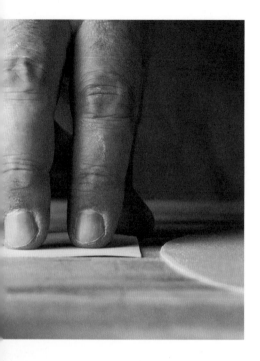

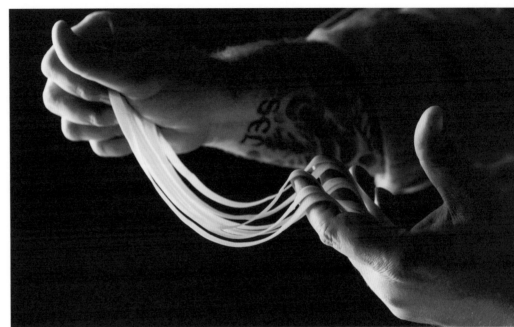

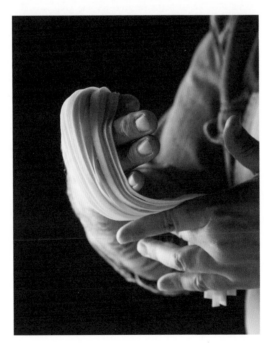

TAGLIATELLE

MAKES ABOUT 710 G [25 OZ], SERVING 6

**1 RECIPE SFOGLIA ALL'UOVO (PAGE 38),
AT ROOM TEMPERATURE**

"00" FLOUR, FOR DUSTING

Roll one dough ball to a thickness of 4 Post-it® Notes on a lightly floured work surface (see page 50). Cure the *sfoglia* (see page 35). Fold the *sfoglia* in half, press gently along the crease, and unfold. Using a sharp knife, cut the *sfoglia* along the crease. Position the half-moon–shaped pieces of *sfoglia* with the round ends closest to you and the cut ends facing away from you. Starting at the round edge of one *sfoglia* crescent, fold the pasta 3 in [7.5 cm] over and continue to fold until you have a loose roll. Repeat with the remaining *sfoglia* crescent.

Beginning at the end of one roll, using a sharp knife, square off the edge and add this irregular shape to your *maltagliati* pile (see page 100). Continue cutting the *sfoglia* crosswise into ¼ in [6 mm] thick strips, adding the irregular rounded edge from the other end of the roll to your *maltagliati* pile. Repeat with the remaining *sfoglia* crescent.

Using one hand, grasp 6 to 8 pasta strands in the middle. Lift them off the work surface and shake to unfurl. With your other hand, grab one end of the dangling strands, invert, and shake to remove excess flour and to separate them from one another. Place the strands on a clean work surface in a horizontal orientation, then form into a U-shape. Repeat with the remaining dough strands. Use now or refrigerate for up to 24 hours in a high-sided container lined with paper towels and loosely covered.

Meanwhile, repeat the process with the remaining dough ball.

If you are planning to dry your tagliatelle in the traditional way, shape them into nests beforehand. Gather 20 to 25 strands, grasping them from the middle, and lift them off the work surface. With your other hand, grab the dangling ends closest to you. Release your other hand and allow the strands to dangle over the top of your fingers. Loosely wrap the strands up and over your hand until they are completely wrapped. Lower the nest onto the work surface and release. Repeat with the remaining strands. When you're ready to cook the nests, simply drop them into boiling salted water.

Everyone's a Critic

My first trip to Bologna, in 2007, was my first trip to Italy. In fact, it was the first time I had traveled anywhere by myself. These were the days of flip phones, long before you could rely on weather apps or Google Maps. I arrived in Bologna by train from Rome, where it had been 75°F [24°C] and sunny. Just a couple hours north, the weather was foggy, overcast, and chilly. I stuck out like a sore thumb in my T-shirt. As I made my way from the station to the apartment I was renting, I saw sincere concern for my well-being in the eyes of passersby—bolognesi, I would later learn, believe underdressing causes illness.

In broken Italian I asked for directions and, eventually, arrived at the front door of my building near Via Stalingrado at the edge of Bologna's red-light district. I buzzed the Buonpensieri apartment where my landlords were supposed to be waiting for me. No answer. This whole Bologna trip wasn't exactly off to a smooth start. After a long, anxiety-filled hour, the Buonpensieris showed up—with Signora Buonpensieri hugging a pile of bedsheets. That made me feel instantly at ease, like I was home.

They showed me to my apartment and we made conversation in hand gestures and my primitive Italian. I told them I had come to study pasta making with the famous Maestra Alessandra. "*Bravo!*" they exclaimed. "But do you know how to cook?" inquired Signora Buonpensieri. I told her I did and she laughed a little too much. "Okay, well maybe we'll try your food sometime," she said, laughing again.

Over the next few months I ran into the Buonpensieris in the hallway and around town. We exchanged pleasantries, but it wasn't until they talked to Maestra Alessandra about me that they invited me to cook dinner for them. Apparently I had gotten Alessandra's coveted seal of approval! They invited me to their country house in Castel Maggiore to cook Sunday dinner. I was ecstatic and I knew just what to make: Tagliatelle al Ragù della Vecchia Scuola (page 90), the *maestra*'s signature dish and go-to comfort food.

Their place was a nice two-story house with a beautiful modern kitchen. I arrived late morning and commenced an epic nine-hour prep session. Signora Buonpensieri left me alone—mostly. Her mother-in-law was much more curious about what I was up to and hovered as I worked. I can't remember having felt more intimidated in a kitchen before, or since. When the time came to make the tagliatelle, I asked for a workspace. Signora Buonpensieri went into the broom closet and brought me a large piece of plywood that had clearly been used thousands of times. I rolled out enough dough to serve 12 people—of course, my landlords had invited their friends to judge the American *sfoglino*.

When the dinner hour came, I plated the tagliatelle and served each guest personally. By that time, I had been in Bologna long enough to know if a native truly disliked something, he or she will leave it on their plate. If they like it, they use a heel of bread to wipe the plate clean. That night, I bussed a dozen spotless dishes from the table. That was all the approval I needed and far more than expected. After dinner, I sat with the Buonpensieris and their friends as they took turns giving their critique or advice. *There wasn't a single compliment in the whole group*, but after that night I could write a thesis on each of their *nonna*'s ragùs.

TAGLIATELLE AL RAGÙ DELLA VECCHIA SCUOLA

TAGLIATELLE WITH MAESTRA ALESSANDRA'S MEAT RAGÙ

Ragù, long-simmered meat sauces, are now synonymous with Bologna and are well into their fifth century on the city's tables. They rose to popularity during the Renaissance, when Italy's nobility began to be heavily influenced by France's spiced stews. And, though you'll never get an Italian to admit it, each ragù is evidence of Francophilia dating back centuries.

Ragù della Vecchia Scuola, the *maestra*'s classic ragù bolognese, tastes of a specific place. The prosciutto, Parmigiano-Reggiano, and vegetables all contribute the characteristics of their own terroir, so, technically, no one can actually recreate Alessandra's ragù outside her city. That doesn't mean I won't try.

An important thing to realize is that if you use products bought in America, or anywhere near you, it won't taste exactly the same as it does in Bologna. But there are tricks to infuse those qualities of bolognese cooking into these dishes. I cook locally and I suggest you do, too. Eighty percent of Italian cooking is about getting the best ingredients. The other 20 percent is about not fucking them up. Buy the best local ingredients you can afford, but know there is no substitute for Parmigiano-Reggiano. It's the backbone of this dish and it's irreplaceable.

You can, however, forgo grinding the meat at home and have your butcher do it for you. You'll have about 2.5 qt [10 cups] of extra sauce when you make this recipe, but trust me, you'll be happy about that.

SERVES 6; MAKES 4 QT/16 CUPS [3.2 KG] SAUCE

2¼ LB [1 KG] BEEF CHUCK, CUT INTO 1 IN [2.5 CM] CUBES

½ LB [227 G] PORK SHOULDER, CUT INTO 1 IN [2.5 CM] CUBES

5 OZ [141 G] PANCETTA, CUT INTO 1 IN [2.5 CM] CUBES

5 OZ [141 G] PROSCIUTTO DI PARMA, CUT INTO 1 IN [2.5 CM] CUBES

5 OZ [141 G] MORTADELLA, CUT INTO 1 IN [2.5 CM] CUBES

4 CELERY STALKS, ROUGHLY CHOPPED

1 CARROT, ROUGHLY CHOPPED

1 LARGE YELLOW ONION, ROUGHLY CHOPPED

5 OZ [140 G] STRUTTO

KOSHER SALT

FRESHLY GROUND BLACK PEPPER

1½ CUPS [360 ML] DRY, FRUITY RED WINE (I LIKE SANGIOVESE)

2 CUPS [450 G] PASSATA DI POMODORO (PAGE 236)

2 CUPS [480 ML] BRODO DI CARNE (PAGE 237), OR LOW-SODIUM CHICKEN BROTH

2 TBSP UNSALTED BUTTER

1 RECIPE TAGLIATELLE (PAGE 88)

1 CUP [100 G] FINELY GRATED PARMIGIANO-REGGIANO

Using a meat grinder, or a grinder attachment, fitted with a large die, grind the beef into a large bowl. Without cleaning the grinder, grind the pork shoulder into the same bowl. Set aside. Without cleaning the grinder, grind the pancetta, prosciutto, and mortadella twice into a medium bowl. Set aside. Pass the celery, carrots, and onions through the grinder into another large bowl and set aside.

In a large heavy-bottomed pot over medium-high heat, melt the *strutto*. Add the ground prosciutto and pancetta and cook until the fat has rendered, about 4 minutes. Add the ground vegetables. Cook, stirring frequently, until they are golden brown and softened, about 15 minutes.

Add the ground beef and pork and generously season with salt and a small amount of pepper. Using a wooden spoon, gently mix the meat and vegetables, stirring from the bottom of the pot. Cook until the meat releases its juices, 6 to 8 minutes. Stir in the wine and cook until the contents of the pan begin to steam. Add the passata and *brodo*, stir to combine, and turn the heat to low.

Cook the sauce at a bare simmer, stirring occasionally, until the meat is tender and the sauce is concentrated, 5 to 7 hours. Begin tasting for tenderness and seasoning after 5 hours. (If you're using grass-fed beef, it will take a lot more time to cook than conventionally raised beef.)

Transfer 6 cups [1.2 kg] of the sauce to a large pot. (Store the extra sauce according to the instructions following.) Place the pan over medium heat. Bring the sauce to a rapid simmer and cook until the sauce reduces slightly, about 3 minutes. Add the butter and swirl to emulsify. Set the sauce aside.

Bring a large pot of water to a rolling boil over high heat. Season the water with salt (see page 25). When the salt dissolves, add the tagliatelle and cook until tender, 30 seconds to 1 minute.

Meanwhile, return the sauce to medium heat. Using a slotted pasta fork, transfer the pasta to the sauce and toss to coat. Add some pasta cooking water, as needed, to loosen the sauce. Serve immediately with the Parmigiano-Reggiano sprinkled on top.

The sauce will keep, refrigerated in an airtight container, for up to 5 days, or frozen for up to 6 months.

TAGLIATELLE IN BIANCO CON PROSCIUTTO CRUDO E BURRO

TAGLIATELLE WITH PROSCIUTTO AND BUTTER

While I was a student at La Vecchia Scuola, we ate tagliatelle dressed with butter-crisped prosciutto at least twice a week. This quick dish was reserved for our busiest days. It's what bolognesi cook when they want comfort food without the time involved in simmering a soulful ragù—and it's perfect for a *laboratorio* churning out pasta at breakneck speed. Alessandra's daughter, Stefania, prepared it using the most delicate local prosciutto, but you can substitute Virginia country ham, if you wish.

SERVES 6

4 TBSP [56 G] UNSALTED BUTTER

4 OZ [113.5 G] PROSCIUTTO DI PARMA, THINLY SLICED AND TORN INTO SLIGHTLY LARGER THAN BITE-SIZE PIECES

KOSHER SALT

1 RECIPE TAGLIATELLE (PAGE 88)

¾ CUP [75 G] FINELY GRATED PARMIGIANO-REGGIANO

In a large sauté pan or skillet over medium heat, melt the butter until frothy and golden. Add the prosciutto. Cook until crispy, about 1 minute. Set the sauce aside.

Bring a large pot of water to a rolling boil over high heat. Season the water with salt (see page 25). When the salt dissolves, add the tagliatelle and cook until tender, 30 seconds to 1 minute.

Meanwhile, return the sauce to medium heat. Using a slotted pasta fork, transfer the pasta to the sauce and toss to coat. Add a splash of pasta cooking water to the pan and swirl vigorously to emulsify. Add ¼ cup [25 g] of the Parmigiano-Reggiano and toss the pasta again. Serve immediately with the remaining Parmigiano-Reggiano sprinkled on top.

TAGLIATELLE CON SALSA DI CIPOLLE

TAGLIATELLE WITH SIMMERED ONIONS

This sauce of "melted" onions has the flavor profile of a rich French onion soup. I have had many versions of this, ranging from a quick, barely cooked sauce of sautéed onions to a luscious, deeply flavored sauce that gains complexity from slow cooking. Marrow bones are available in some butcher shops. If you can't find them, omit them, but the result won't be quite as richly delicious. If you substitute beef consommé for the Brodo di Carne, reduce the salt to 1 Tbsp.

SERVES 6

6 TBSP [84 G] STRUTTO

THREE 3 IN [7.5 CM] LONG MARROW BONES, CUT CROSSWISE

8 OZ [227 G] PANCETTA, FINELY DICED

2½ LB [1.1 KG] SHALLOTS, PEELED AND THINLY SLICED

10 LARGE YELLOW ONIONS, THINLY SLICED

2 TBSP KOSHER SALT, PLUS MORE FOR SEASONING

1 TBSP FRESHLY GROUND BLACK PEPPER

2 CUPS [480 ML] DRY WHITE WINE

3 CUPS [480 ML] BRODO DI CARNE (PAGE 237), OR BEEF CONSOMMÉ

1 RECIPE TAGLIATELLE (PAGE 88)

1 CUP [100 G] FINELY GRATED PARMIGIANO-REGGIANO

In a large heavy-bottomed pot over medium heat, melt the *strutto*. Add the bones and cook on all sides until golden brown and the marrow begins to weep out, about 6 minutes total.

Decrease the heat to low. Carefully shake the marrow from the bones into the pot. It should be loose and come out easily. If it resists, use the end of a spoon to push it out. Discard the bones. Add the pancetta and cook, stirring occasionally, until crispy and golden brown and the fat has rendered, about 5 minutes. Add the shallots, onions, salt, and pepper and stir to combine.

Increase the heat to medium and cover the pot. Cook until the shallots and onions are very soft and golden, about 1 hour, stirring every 10 minutes. If the onions stick to the bottom of the pot, remove the pot from the heat and let sit, still covered, for 3 to 5 minutes. The onions will naturally release from the pot. Stir, scraping the bottom of the pot, and return it to the heat.

Increase the heat to high and uncover the pot. Cook until the onions are juicy and jammy and browned, 30 to 45 minutes. Add the wine and cook until the alcohol aroma dissipates and the liquid has reduced by half, about

6 minutes. Add the *brodo* and cook, stirring frequently, until the onions are once again juicy and jammy and the liquid has reduced by one fourth, about 15 minutes. Set the sauce aside.

Bring a large pot of water to a rolling boil over high heat. Season the water with salt (see page 25). When the salt dissolves, add the tagliatelle and cook until tender, 30 seconds to 1 minute.

Meanwhile, return the sauce to medium heat. Using a slotted pasta fork, transfer the pasta to the sauce and toss to coat. Add a splash of pasta cooking water to the pan and swirl vigorously to emulsify. Add ¼ cup [25 g] of the Parmigiano-Reggiano and toss the pasta again. Serve immediately with the remaining Parmigiano-Reggiano sprinkled on top.

The sauce will keep, refrigerated in an airtight container, for up to 5 days.

MALTAG

Maltagliati translates as "badly cut" and refers to the irregularly shaped pasta bits left over when you cut tagliatelle, pappardelle, or other shapes that yield scraps. Back in the day, maltagliati were simply a by-product of pasta production. These days, you still find them on trattoria menus as an item that lets the kitchen use up leftover pasta bits—but they can also be made purposefully.

I had heard of maltagliati before landing in Bologna almost 10 years ago, but what stuck with me was maltagliati's role in Bologna's sense of community. La Vecchia Scuola was in a poorer part of town and Alessandra would save scraps from the students' sfoglie, dry them, bag them, and give them away to people in the neighborhood. It was a beautiful thing.

LIATI

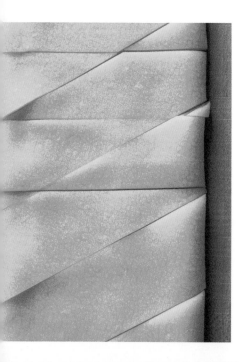

MALTAGLIATI

MAKES ABOUT 710 G [25 OZ], SERVING 6

1 RECIPE SFOGLIA ALL'UOVO (PAGE 38),
AT ROOM TEMPERATURE

"00" FLOUR, FOR DUSTING

Roll one dough ball to a thickness of 9 Post-it® Notes on a lightly floured work surface (see page 50). Cure the *sfoglia* (see page 35). Fold the *sfoglia* in half, press gently along the crease, and unfold. Using a sharp knife, cut the *sfoglia* along the crease. Position the half-moon–shaped pieces of *sfoglia* with the round ends closest to you and the cut ends facing away from you. Starting at the round edge of one *sfoglia* crescent, fold the pasta 3 in [7.5 cm] over and continue to fold until you have a loose roll. Repeat with the remaining dough. Beginning at the end of one roll, using a sharp knife, cut the dough into 1 in [2.5 cm] thick strips. Cut each strip 1 in [2.5 cm] diagonally. Repeat with the remaining dough.

Using both hands, gather up the dough pieces and gently toss them to separate the pieces, setting them down on a clean work surface. The *maltagliati* are ready to use now, or you can dry them for future use: Set aside on a wooden surface, at room temperature, until completely dry, 2 to 3 hours. You can expedite the drying process by placing a fan near the pasta, avoiding direct air.

Meanwhile, repeat the process with the remaining dough ball.

The dried pasta will keep, at room temperature in an airtight container, for up to 2 weeks or frozen for up to 6 months.

MALTAGLIATI PILE

When bolognesi make a recipe featuring *maltagliati*, they use the scraps they generate from making other pasta shapes. This practice is ideal in terms of practicality and economy, ensuring none of the dough goes to waste—and you get a bonus meal out of it. So, whenever you make any type of pasta, don't throw away the odds and ends remaining after you've rolled and cut the dough. Instead, set them aside on a porous surface at room temperature until completely dry, 2 to 3 hours. They will keep, at room temperature in an airtight container, for up to 2 weeks or frozen for up to 6 months. Keep adding to your stash and cook the pasta when you've accumulated enough for your needs. Obviously here I give instructions for making *maltagliati* from scratch, so the shape of the pasta pieces will be uniform. The recipe calls for Sfoglia all'Uovo but you can absolutely substitute Sfoglia di Acqua e Farina (page 34).

MALTAGLIATI CON FAGIOLI

MALTAGLIATI WITH BEANS

Pasta *e fagioli* (with beans) is an Italian farmhouse classic found in virtually every region of Italy. The beans of choice in Bologna are the *borlotti* (cranberry beans), but you can substitute navy beans, cannellini beans, or even chick-peas. As with the ragù recipes, you can use the sauce right away, but I think it's improved after sitting in the refrigerator overnight or for up to 3 days. Just be sure to let it cool completely before refrigerating and keep it tightly covered.

SERVES 6

8 TBSP [1 STICK, OR 112 G] UNSALTED BUTTER

1 THICK SLICE (3½ OZ [100 G]) PROSCIUTTO

ONE 3 IN [7.5 CM] SPRIG ROSEMARY

3 GARLIC CLOVES, SMASHED

ONE 3 IN [7.5 CM] PARMIGIANO-REGGIANO RIND

1 CUP [240 ML] DRY WHITE WINE

2 QT [1.9 L] COLD WATER

8 OZ (1 CUP [227 G]) DRIED BORLOTTI BEANS, SOAKED IN WATER OVERNIGHT (SEE TIP) AND DRAINED

KOSHER SALT

2 TBSP STRUTTO

3 TBSP CHOPPED FRESH FLAT-LEAF PARSLEY

2 CUPS [450 G] PASSATA DI POMODORO (PAGE 236)

1 RECIPE MALTAGLIATI (PAGE 100), OR 700 G [ABOUT 1½ LB] PASTA FROM YOUR MALTAGLIATI PILE (SEE PAGE 100)

1 CUP [100 G] FINELY GRATED PARMIGIANO-REGGIANO

In a large heavy-bottomed pot over medium heat, melt the butter until frothy and golden. Add the prosciutto and cook until browned, about 2 minutes. Add the rosemary, 2 garlic cloves, and the Parmigiano-Reggiano rind and cook until the garlic turns golden, about 4 minutes, stirring frequently to prevent the rind from sticking to the bottom of the pot.

Add the wine and bring the mixture to a boil. Cook until the alcohol aroma dissipates and the liquid has reduced by half, about 2 minutes. Add the cold water and return the mixture to a boil. Stir in the beans, decrease the heat to low, and cover the pot. Simmer until the beans are tender, about 1 hour, stirring every 10 minutes or so. Remove the pot from the heat and let the beans rest for 15 minutes. Remove and discard the prosciutto, rosemary, and Parmigiano-Reggiano rind. Heavily season the bean mixture with salt.

In another large heavy-bottomed pot over medium heat, melt the *strutto*. Add the remaining garlic clove and the parsley and cook just until the garlic takes color, about 30 seconds. Add the *passata* and bring the sauce to a rapid simmer. Add the cooked beans and 4 cups [960 ml] of the cooking liquid and season with salt. Bring the mixture to a boil, then add the *maltagliati*, stirring to separate the pieces. Cook until the pasta is tender, about 3 minutes. Stir in ½ cup [50 g] of the Parmigiano-Reggiano and serve immediately with the remaining Parmigiano-Reggiano on the side.

To prepare dried beans, place them in a large container with three times their volume of water. Cover and soak in the refrigerator overnight. Rinse and drain them before using.

MALTAGLIATI CON "JEDA"

MALTAGLIATI WITH WALNUT PESTO

Jeda is, essentially, a walnut and garlic pesto that's a staple of *la cucina povera*–poor people's cooking–in the Apennine Mountains that border southern Bologna. Some versions throw in boiled potatoes, which were a welcome addition for the hungry peasants working the fields; they needed every last morsel and calorie they could get. I prefer a lighter approach, so I omit them.

SERVES 6

2 CUPS [240 G] WALNUT HALVES

2 GARLIC CLOVES

**5½ OZ [150 G] PANCETTA,
CUT INTO ¼ IN [6 MM] BATONS**

1 SPRIG FRESH ROSEMARY

KOSHER SALT

**1 RECIPE MALTAGLIATI (PAGE 100), OR
700 G [ABOUT 1½ LB] PASTA FROM YOUR
MALTAGLIATI PILE (SEE PAGE 100)**

**1½ CUPS [150 G] FINELY GRATED
PARMIGIANO-REGGIANO**

Preheat the oven to 300°F [150°C]. Line a baking sheet with parchment paper.

Spread the walnuts evenly over the prepared baking sheet and toast until mahogany colored, about 10 minutes. Transfer to the bowl of a food processor, add the garlic, and pulse until the walnuts are the size of peas, about 1 minute.

In a large skillet over medium heat, cook the pancetta, stirring occasionally, until crispy and the fat has rendered, about 3 minutes. Fry the whole sprig of rosemary in the rendered fat until fragrant, about 30 seconds. Remove to a plate and set aside to cool, then pick the leaves and set aside. Discard the stem. Stir the walnut mixture into the rendered fat in the skillet. Set the sauce aside.

Bring a large pot of water to a rolling boil over high heat. Season the water with salt (see page 25). When the salt dissolves, add the *maltagliati* and stir to separate the pieces. Cook until tender, about 2 minutes.

Meanwhile, return the sauce to medium heat. Using a spider, transfer the pasta and a splash of the pasta cooking water to the sauce. Stir vigorously to emulsify. Add additional pasta cooking water, as needed, to loosen the sauce. Stir in ½ cup [50 g] of the Parmigiano-Reggiano and serve immediately with the remaining Parmigiano-Reggiano sprinkled on top. Garnish with the rosemary.

MALTAGLIATI CON BATTUTO DI ERBE SELVATICHE

MALTAGLIATI WITH WILD HERB PESTO

The bolognese approach to this dish, one that evokes the wild flavors of the hills around the city, would be to boil everything together before chopping it all up. I prefer to give the ingredients a little more love, cooking the herbs first then sautéing the greens in the same pan. This creates a greater depth of flavor and helps compensate for the milder-tasting farm-grown herbs we tend to find in the States and elsewhere.

SERVES 6

1½ CUPS [360 ML] EXTRA-VIRGIN OLIVE OIL

1 GARLIC CLOVE, SMASHED

½ CUP [6 G] LOOSELY PACKED FRESH MINT LEAVES

4 FRESH SAGE LEAVES

2 TBSP FRESH MARJORAM LEAVES

FRONDS FROM 1 FENNEL BULB

4 OZ [113.5 G] DANDELION GREENS, OR RADICCHIO, TORN

4 OZ [113.5 G] RAPINI (BROCCOLI RABE), TORN

4 OZ [113.5 G] WATERCRESS, TORN

4 OZ [113.5 G] TURNIP GREENS

4 OZ [113.5 G] ARUGULA, TORN

KOSHER SALT

FRESHLY GROUND BLACK PEPPER

¼ CUP [60 ML] DRY WHITE WINE

3 TBSP UNSALTED BUTTER

1 RECIPE MALTAGLIATI (PAGE 100), OR 700 G (ABOUT 1½ LB) PASTA FROM YOUR MALTAGLIATI PILE (SEE PAGE 100)

½ CUP [50 G] GRATED PECORINO ROMANO

In a large pot over medium heat, heat the oil until it begins to shimmer. Add the garlic and cook until fragrant, about 1 minute. Add the mint, sage, marjoram, and fennel fronds and cook until aromatic, about 45 seconds.

Add the dandelion greens, rapini leaves, watercress, turnip greens, and arugula, season with salt and pepper, and cook, stirring frequently, until wilted, about 4 minutes. Add the wine and cook until the greens are very tender, about 10 minutes. Remove from the heat and spread the mixture on a cutting board, reserving the pot and the liquid in it.

After about 10 minutes, when the greens and herbs are cool enough to handle, chop everything into small pieces. Alternatively, transfer them to the bowl of a food processor and pulse. Return the pot to medium heat and add the butter to melt. Add the chopped greens and herbs and stir to coat. Set the sauce aside.

Bring a large pot of water to a rolling boil over high heat. Season the water with salt (see page 25). When the salt dissolves, add the *maltagliati* and stir to separate the pieces. Cook until tender, about 2 minutes.

Meanwhile, return the sauce to medium heat. Using a spider, transfer the pasta to the sauce and stir to coat. Add some pasta cooking water, as needed, to loosen the sauce. Serve immediately with the cheese sprinkled on top.

Tasting the Flavors of the Colline Bolognesi

Savigno is a 40-minute drive from Bologna, over rolling country roads into the heart of the Colline Bolognesi (the hills outside Bologna). Upon arrival, a kitschy sign welcomes visitors to the "Town of Tartufo," a reference to Savigno's main industry—truffle hunting (see page 225). The beige and pastel-hued town center isn't much more than a main street flanked by porticoes, a church, and a parking lot, but it looms large in my culinary memories thanks to Amerigo dal 1934.

Amerigo Bettini opened his eponymous trattoria in, yes, 1934. For many years, it was the town's main draw, aside from the truffle hunting. I wasn't fortunate enough to dine there under his reign, but his grandson Alberto, who took over from his father about 10 years ago, is doing wonderful things there. The rustic restaurant and food shop, which had seen better days, has once again become a dining destination that attracts chefs and culinary travelers from all over the world. Alberto claims his version of Amerigo is modern, but I feel as though the soulful dishes now served in the trattoria's five rooms are quite restrained. The plating is, perhaps, a bit contemporary, but the flavors on the plate are classic.

If you visit Amerigo, I suggest starting with *tigelle* (soft disks of fried bread) draped with thinly sliced cured meats. Then move on to one of the planet's most satisfying dishes, *tortelli* filled with crema di Parmigiano-Reggiano, liquefied salted cow's milk cheese. Don't skip the tortellini, which are served in a savory broth as tradition demands; they are so tiny you can fit eight on a soupspoon. Seasonal truffles appear throughout the year: black spring or summer truffles are grated over fried eggs or pasta; in autumn and winter, *uova Amerigo*—egg soufflé with a flurry of white truffle shavings—is the way to go. For dessert, try the ricotta drizzled with *saba*, a local grape molasses that delivers a sweet counterpoint to the cheese's savory tang. Whenever I linger over coffee and grappa under the same wooden beams, vintage light fixtures, and wrought iron decorations that Amerigo installed himself, I contemplate how even just a 40-minute drive can transport you to a different, but connected, food culture.

STRICH

Strichetti is Alessandra's name for a pasta shape you probably know as farfalle (butterflies) for its distinctive winged form. This is a fairly modern pasta shape, which became popular in the 1970s and, in Bologna, you're·likely to find the dried form sold in boxes; only a handful of pasta workshops make *strichetti* by hand.

My approach here illuminates, perhaps better than any other shape in the book, the architectural and structural view I take of pasta. When cooked, most *strichetti* are crunchy in the middle and overcooked on the sides due to improper pinching at the pasta's touch points. Due to their folds, it's tough to cook a piece to a universally tender texture. I have re-engineered the pasta shaping itself to ensure even cooking. By pinching *strichetti* my way, the dough forms a canal, of sorts, that lets the water flow freely around the pasta, ensuring a universally tender piece every time.

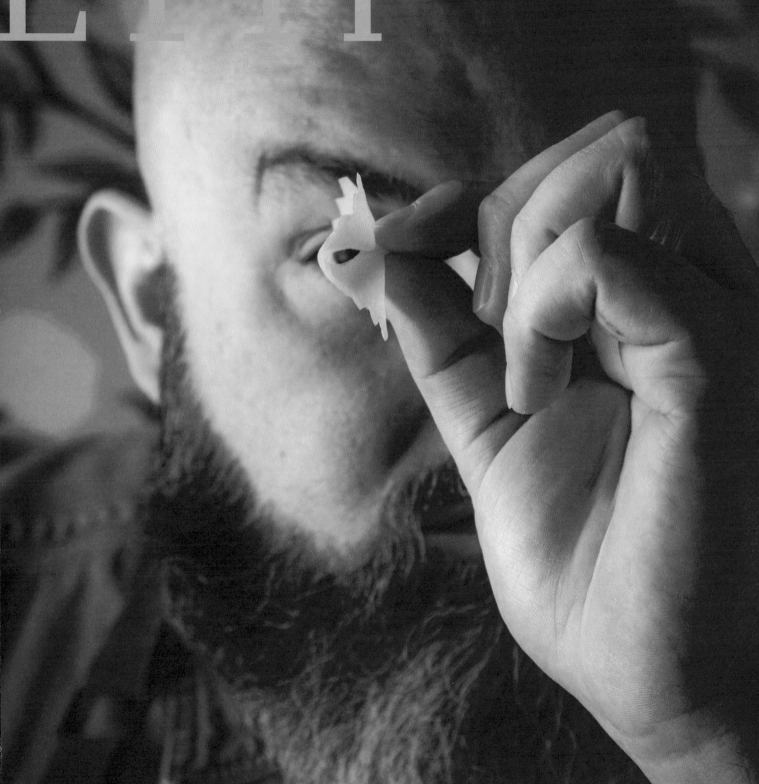

STRICHETTI

MAKES ABOUT 710 G [25 OZ],
SERVING 6

**1 RECIPE SFOGLIA ALL'UOVO (PAGE 38),
AT ROOM TEMPERATURE**

"00" FLOUR, FOR DUSTING

Roll one dough ball to a thickness of 7 Post-it® Notes on a lightly floured work surface (see page 50). Set an accordion pastry cutter to 2 in [5 cm]. Beginning at the bottom of the *sfoglia*, cut from east to west, creating 2 in [5 cm] strips. Using a fluted pastry cutter, cut the *sfoglia* strips south to north into 3 in [7.5 cm] pieces. If you don't have a fluted pastry cutter, use the accordion pastry cutter to cut the *sfoglia* into 3 in [7.5 cm] pieces. Clear away any scraps and add them to your *maltagliati* pile (see page 100).

Cover the *sfoglia* with a clean, unscented plastic trash can liner, leaving the first row, closest to you, exposed. Position your index finger in the center of a pasta piece. Position your thumb and middle finger in line with the index finger at the bottom and top edge of the pasta piece, respectively. Gather the top and bottom edges and move them toward your index finger, creating two folds forming a valley with your index finger. Release your index finger and pinch only the peaks of the pasta together, ensuring a single thickness (see page 24) at the connection. This will create a tube through the middle of the shape, beneath the closure. Repeat with the remaining pasta pieces.

Transfer the shaped pasta to a clean work surface and let dry, uncovered, at room temperature, for 10 to 15 minutes. The *strichetti* are now ready to use, or you can dry them for future use: Set aside on a wooden surface, at room temperature, until completely dry, 2 to 3 hours. You can expedite the drying process by placing a fan near the pasta, avoiding direct air.

Meanwhile, repeat the process with the remaining dough ball.

The dried pasta will keep, at room temperature in an airtight container, for up to 2 weeks.

STRICHETTI ALLA ROMAGNOLA

STRICHETTI WITH PROSCIUTTO, ARUGULA, AND TOMATOES

Romagna is the often-overlooked neighbor to the east of Emilia. While it is home to beach resorts, such as Rimini and Riccione, its cuisine is definitely overshadowed by the globally revered food of Bologna, Modena, and Parma. That said, the dishes of Romagna are simple, satisfying, and easy to prepare, and this pasta is no exception. This is exactly the kind of dish I want to eat on the beach in Rimini, packed into a Tupperware™ and devoured at ambient temperature while sprawled under a beach umbrella.

SERVES 6

4 TBSP [56 G] UNSALTED BUTTER

5 OZ [140 G] PROSCIUTTO DI PARMA, THINLY SLICED AND TORN INTO SLIGHTLY LARGER THAN BITE-SIZE PIECES

1½ PT [ABOUT 18 OZ, OR 510 G] CHERRY TOMATOES

KOSHER SALT

4 OZ [113.5 G] ARUGULA, PLUS MORE FOR GARNISHING

1 RECIPE STRICHETTI (PAGE 112)

1 CUP [100 G] FINELY GRATED PARMIGIANO-REGGIANO

In a large pot over medium heat, melt the butter until frothy and golden. Add the prosciutto and cook until aromatic, about 15 seconds. Add the cherry tomatoes and season with salt. Cook just until softened. Add the arugula and toss to combine. Set the sauce aside.

Bring a large pot of water to a rolling boil over high heat. Season the water with salt (see page 25). When the salt dissolves, add the *strichetti* and cook until tender, 2½ to 3 minutes.

Meanwhile, return the sauce to medium heat. Using a spider, transfer the pasta to the sauce. Add about 2 Tbsp of pasta cooking water and toss vigorously to coat. Serve immediately with the Parmigiano-Reggiano sprinkled on top.

STRICHETTI CON PROSCIUTTO COTTO E PISELLI

STRICHETTI WITH HAM AND PEAS

Like Strichetti alla Romagnola (page 114), this is another supremely simple dish. It combines ham and peas and is scented with sage, which grows wild all over Bologna and its outskirts. It's the quintessential spring dish. If you want to make it outside of pea season, use frozen peas or even snap peas instead of fresh English peas. I use Italian *prosciutto cotto* (cooked cured ham), but you can substitute Virginia country ham or a good quality deli ham, as long as it's not flavored.

SERVES 6

4 TBSP [56 G] UNSALTED BUTTER

4 FRESH SAGE LEAVES

8 OZ [227 G] COOKED HAM, FINELY DICED

2 CUPS [300 G] SHELLED ENGLISH PEAS, BLANCHED

KOSHER SALT

1 RECIPE STRICHETTI (PAGE 112)

1 CUP [100 G] FINELY GRATED PARMIGIANO-REGGIANO

In a large sauté pan or skillet over medium heat, melt the butter until frothy and golden. Add the sage and ham and cook until the ham is golden brown, about 30 seconds. Add the peas and cook just until warmed through, about 45 seconds. Season with salt and set the sauce aside.

Bring a large pot of water to a rolling boil over high heat. Season the water with salt (see page 25). When the salt dissolves, add the *strichetti* and cook until tender, 2½ to 3 minutes.

Meanwhile, return the sauce to medium heat. Using a spider, transfer the pasta to the sauce and stir to coat. Add 2 Tbsp of pasta cooking water and swirl to emulsify. Serve immediately with the Parmigiano-Reggiano sprinkled on top.

Mortadella

For me, mortadella defines Bologna. This cooked salami, made from an assortment of mashed pork cuts studded with fat, is not just delicious but also super versatile. It's served as is, thinly sliced or cubed and spiked with a toothpick, whipped into a *spuma* (mousse), roasted, grilled, poached in broth, ground into meatballs, folded into tortellini fillings (see page 178), and in countless other ways, including in Strichetti con Mortadella e Panna (see facing page).

Beyond its flavors and omnipresence, what I love most about Bologna's iconic salami is its mythology. Ask any bolognese person and he or she will tell you it has been made in Emilia-Romagna for thousands of years, since Etruscan times. I learned pretty early on that it pays to be skeptical of Italian claims like this. The fact is, a lot of what is eaten in Italy today is either modern (Renaissance or newer) or vaguely similar to something made in the Middle Ages or antiquity. Yet, I guarantee, if you ask a salami maker, deli owner, or home cook about mortadella, they will detail its ancient origins as pure fact.

What we do know is how mortadella is made today and how it is defined by law. The process is implied by its name: *mortare* means to smash or pulverize, as with a mortar and pestle. The mashed pork is mixed with cubes of pork fat, stuffed into casings, and slowly baked in dry-air ovens to produce a delicate flavor and velvety texture.

Mortadella di Bologna is protected by an IGP (*Indicazione Geografica Protetta*) seal, which means the area in and methods with which it is made are defined by official law. IGP rules are quite a bit looser than the DOP regulations that protect prosciutto di Parma (see page 250); while the latter are made in a very small area around Parma, mortadella di Bologna IGP can be made in Emilia-Romagna and seven other regions, including Lombardy, Veneto, Le Marche, Piedmont, Tuscany, Lazio, and Trentino. The IGP also stipulates the salami must be made from a ground paste of whole pork muscles with the addition of at least 15 percent fat cubes cut from around the pork neck and collar. Flavorings may include black peppercorns or whole shelled pistachios. Mortadella lovers have—and are passionate about—their preferences. Once Maestra Alessandra received a delivery of mortadella studded with pistachios and she berated the purveyor so intensely I'm sure he never made that mistake again!

STRICHETTI CON MORTADELLA E PANNA

STRICHETTI WITH MORTADELLA AND CREAM

I fucking love mortadella. In Bologna, this salami refuses to be outshined by Parma's globally celebrated prosciutto. *Strichetti* with mortadella and cream is the ultimate comfort food for a cold Bologna night—and one I whipped up more than a few times after getting home late from a night out at a bar. The mortadella gets a little crispy on the outside when you fry it in the butter and it returns the favor, "seasoning" the butter by weeping out its delicately spiced flavors.

SERVES 6

3 TBSP [42 G] UNSALTED BUTTER

12 OZ [340 G] MORTADELLA, CUT INTO ½ IN [12 MM] CUBES

1½ CUPS [360 ML] HEAVY CREAM

KOSHER SALT

FRESHLY GROUND BLACK PEPPER

1 RECIPE STRICHETTI (PAGE 112)

1 CUP [100 G] FINELY GRATED PARMIGIANO-REGGIANO

In a large sauté pan or skillet over medium heat, melt the butter until frothy and golden. Add the mortadella and cook until golden brown, about 45 seconds. Add the cream, bring to a rapid simmer, and cook until reduced by half, about 3 minutes. Season with salt and pepper. Set the sauce aside.

Bring a large pot of water to a rolling boil over high heat. Season the water with salt (see page 25). When the salt dissolves, add the *strichetti* and cook until tender, 2½ to 3 minutes.

Meanwhile, return the sauce to medium heat. Using a spider, transfer the pasta to the sauce and stir to coat. Add 2 Tbsp of pasta cooking water and swirl to emulsify. Add ¼ cup [25 g] of the Parmigiano-Reggiano and mix until incorporated. Serve immediately with the remaining Parmigiano-Reggiano sprinkled on top.

GARGAN

Spago in Beverly Hills is where my love of pasta began taking shape. There, *garganelli* were handmade every day by Esse, one of the most methodical cooks I have ever worked with. He was ornery but efficient and he would churn out thousands of pieces of pasta in a service. Among them was *garganelli*, a ridged tube-shaped pasta and one of the few in this book that requires special equipment. The textured surface of the pasta helps sauce cling to it.

To create the characteristic ridges, purchase a *pettina* (pasta comb) in Bologna or online. Alternatively, use a sushi mat or inexpensive gnocchi board—both will leave the signature ridged impressions in the dough as you roll it around a thin dowel. In Italy, *pettine* come with dowels, but you can improvise. Esse used a Sharpie™ with the pocket clip snapped off and his method worked like a charm.

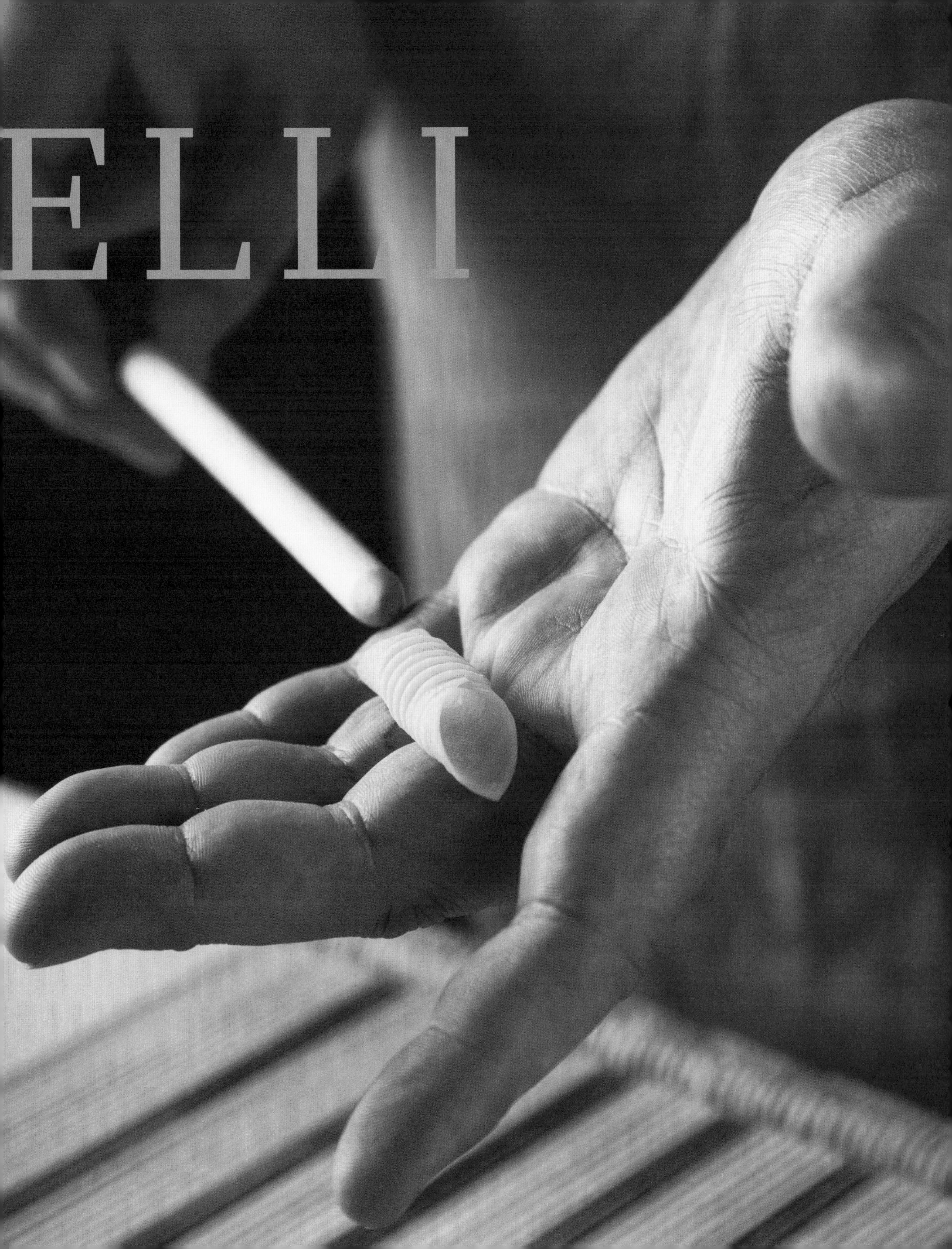
ELLI

GARGANELLI

MAKES ABOUT 710 G [25 OZ], SERVING 6

1 RECIPE SFOGLIA ALL'UOVO (PAGE 38),
AT ROOM TEMPERATURE

"00" FLOUR, FOR DUSTING

Roll one dough ball to a thickness of 4 Post-it® Notes on a lightly floured work surface (see page 50). Set it aside on your work surface, uncovered, for 2 to 3 minutes to dry slightly. Cover the *sfoglia* with plastic and let rest for 2 to 3 minutes more.

Set an accordion pastry cutter to 1½ in [4 cm]. Use firm and even pressure to cut the *sfoglia* into strips, moving from south to north. The edge of the pastry cutter should graze the east edge of the *sfoglia*. Beginning at the bottom edge of the *sfoglia*, use firm and even pressure to cut the dough into strips, east to west. Clear away any scraps and add them to your *maltagliati* pile (see page 100).

Cover the *sfoglia* with a clean, unscented plastic trash can liner, leaving the first row, closest to you, exposed. Position the *pettina* on your work surface. Transfer a square of pasta to the *pettina*, oriented in a diamond shape. Place the dowel at the bottom third of the diamond. Wrap the southern tip of the pasta over the dowel. Using your index fingers, apply firm pressure to the dowel and press down and away from you, wrapping the pasta in a cylinder around the dowel. Repeat with the remaining pasta pieces.

Transfer the shaped pasta to a clean work surface and let dry, uncovered, for 30 to 40 minutes. The *garganelli* are now ready to use, or you can dry them for future use: Set aside on a wooden surface, at room temperature, until completely dry, 2 to 3 hours. You can expedite the drying process by placing a fan near the pasta, avoiding direct air.

Meanwhile, repeat the process with the remaining dough ball.

The dried pasta will keep, at room temperature in an airtight container, for up to 2 weeks.

GARGANELLI IN BIANCO CON SALSICCIA E CARDI

GARGANELLI WITH SAUSAGE AND CARDOONS

In late fall and winter, vegetable gardens in Bologna pop off with hearty produce, such as cardoons, which can survive cold snaps and freezing weather. This variety of thistle is related to the artichoke and shares with it a sweet nuttiness. It is a natural pairing with sausage, as it is harvested at about the same time the traditional pig slaughter occurs. When preparing this recipe, use any sweet Italian sausage you like, as long as it is not flavored with fennel, which would compete with the delicate flavor of the cardoons.

SERVES 6

4 OZ [113.5 G] PANCETTA,
CUT INTO ¼ INCH [6 MM] BATONS

4 SWEET ITALIAN SAUSAGE LINKS (ABOUT
1 LB [454 G] TOTAL), CASINGS REMOVED

1 LARGE YELLOW ONION, DICED

4 (8.5 OZ [240 G]) BLANCHED CARDOONS
(SEE SIDEBAR)

KOSHER SALT

FRESHLY GROUND BLACK PEPPER

½ CUP [120 ML] DRY WHITE WINE

2 CUPS [480 ML] BRODO DI CARNE
(PAGE 237), OR LOW-SODIUM CHICKEN BROTH

1 RECIPE GARGANELLI (PAGE 124)

1 CUP [100 G] FINELY GRATED
PARMIGIANO-REGGIANO

In a large sauté pan or skillet over medium-high heat, cook the pancetta until the fat has rendered, about 4 minutes. Add the sausage and cook, breaking it apart with a wooden spoon, until golden brown, 4 to 5 minutes. Add the onion and cardoons, season with salt and pepper, and cook until the onion is translucent, about 8 minutes.

Add the wine and cook until it evaporates, about 2 minutes. Add the *brodo* and bring to a boil. Decrease the heat to low and simmer until the cardoons are very tender and the broth is reduced by half, about 20 minutes. Set the sauce aside.

Bring a large pot of water to a rolling boil over high heat. Season the water with salt (see page 25). When the salt dissolves, add the *garganelli* and cook until tender, 2½ to 3 minutes.

Meanwhile, return the sauce to medium heat. Using a spider, transfer the pasta to the sauce and stir to coat. Add some pasta cooking water, as needed, to loosen the sauce. Serve immediately with the Parmigiano-Reggiano sprinkled on top.

BLANCHED CARDOONS

Blanching cardoons before cooking them gets rid of their bitterness and astrigency. Unlike with traditional blanching, here there is no need to shock the vegetables in ice water to stop the cooking and preserve the color.

JUICE OF 1 LEMON

4 CARDOON STALKS

KOSHER SALT

Fill a large bowl with cold water and add the lemon juice. Set aside. Using a paring knife and working from top to bottom, trim and discard each fibrous raised rib from the cardoon stalks. Cut the stalks crosswise into ¼ in [6 mm] pieces and place them in the bowl with the lemon water to prevent them from oxidizing.

Bring a large pot of water to a rolling boil over high heat. Season the water with salt (see page 25). When the salt dissolves, add the cardoons. Cook until tender, about 4 minutes. Drain.

The cardoons will keep, refrigerated in an airtight container, for up to 3 days.

GARGANELLI AI PEPERONI

GARGANELLI WITH BELL PEPPERS

This is a rare vegetarian dish in a sea of meaty bolognese delights—in fact, you can even turn the dish vegan by using the egg-free *strozzapreti* (see page 232) in place of the *garganelli* and omitting the cheese. The recipe employs simmered peppers and onions, a classic summer side dish called *peperonata*, as a pasta sauce. If you can't find lunchbox peppers, use Jimmy Nardello peppers.

SERVES 6

½ CUP [120 ML] EXTRA-VIRGIN OLIVE OIL

2 GARLIC CLOVES, SMASHED

20 FRESH BASIL LEAVES, TORN

10 SPRIGS MARJORAM, LEAVES REMOVED

1 LARGE BUNCH FRESH FLAT-LEAF PARSLEY, CHOPPED

1 YELLOW ONION, THINLY SLICED

1 SMALL FENNEL BULB, OUTER LAYER DISCARDED, THINLY SLICED

KOSHER SALT

2 LB [907 G] SMALL YELLOW AND RED LUNCHBOX PEPPERS OR JIMMY NARDELLO PEPPERS (20 TO 25), CORED AND THINLY SLICED

1 RECIPE GARGANELLI (PAGE 124)

1 CUP [100 G] FINELY GRATED PARMIGIANO-REGGIANO

In a large pot over medium heat, heat the oil until it begins to shimmer. Add the garlic and cook just until fragrant, about 30 seconds, then discard the garlic. Add the basil, marjoram, and parsley and cook, swirling, for 1 minute. Add the onion and fennel, season with salt, and cook until the onion softens, about 7 minutes. Add the peppers, season with salt, and cook until they are very soft, juicy, and jammy, about 15 minutes. Set the sauce aside.

Bring a large pot of water to a rolling boil over high heat. Season the water with salt (see page 25). When the salt dissolves, add the *garganelli* and cook until tender, 2½ to 3 minutes.

Return the sauce to medium heat. Using a spider, transfer the pasta to the sauce and stir to coat. Add some pasta cooking water, as needed, to loosen the sauce. Serve immediately with the Parmigiano-Reggiano sprinkled on top.

The sauce will keep, refrigerated in an airtight container, for up to 5 days.

GARGANELLI CON RAGÙ DI AGNELLO

GARGANELLI WITH LAMB RAGÙ

This braised lamb ragù is an Easter specialty in Emilia-Romagna, marrying the Christian symbolism of the sacrificial lamb with the natural rhythms of nature. In Bologna, suckling lambs are slaughtered in spring just as peas come into season. The tender meat is simmered with herbs and sweet seasonal peas, resulting in a soulful sauce with deep flavor. If you don't have access to fresh peas, substitute frozen. You can use the sauce right away, but I think it's improved after sitting in the refrigerator overnight, or for up to 3 days. Just be sure to let it cool completely before refrigerating and keep it tightly covered.

SERVES 6; MAKES 4 QT/16 CUPS [3.2 KG] SAUCE

3 LB [1.4 KG] LAMB SHOULDER, CUT INTO 1 IN [2.5 CM] CUBES

5 OZ [141 G] PANCETTA, CUT INTO 1 IN [2.5 CM] CUBES

4 CELERY STALKS, ROUGHLY CHOPPED

1 LARGE YELLOW ONION, ROUGHLY CHOPPED

1 LARGE CARROT, ROUGHLY CHOPPED

1 SMALL FENNEL BULB, ROUGHLY CHOPPED

1¼ CUPS [300 ML] EXTRA-VIRGIN OLIVE OIL

5 FRESH SAGE LEAVES, TORN

2 GARLIC CLOVES, MINCED

1 SPRIG ROSEMARY, LEAVES REMOVED

1 BAY LEAF, PREFERABLY FRESH

1 TBSP TOMATO PASTE

KOSHER SALT

FRESHLY GROUND BLACK PEPPER

1½ CUPS [360 ML] DRY RED WINE

3 CUPS [675 G] PASSATA DI POMODORO (PAGE 236)

2 CUPS [450 G] BRODO DI CARNE (PAGE 237), OR LOW-SODIUM CHICKEN BROTH

2 TBSP UNSALTED BUTTER

1 RECIPE GARGANELLI (PAGE 124)

1 CUP [100 G] FINELY GRATED PECORINO ROMANO

Using a meat grinder, or a grinder attachment, fitted with a large die, grind the lamb shoulder into a large bowl and set aside. Without cleaning the grinder, grind the pancetta into a small bowl and set aside. Grind the celery, onions, carrot, and fennel into a separate large bowl and set aside.

In a large heavy-bottomed pot over medium heat, heat the oil until it begins to shimmer. Add the ground pancetta and cook until the fat has rendered, about 1 minute. Add the sage, garlic, rosemary, and bay leaf and cook until fragrant, about 20 seconds. Add the ground vegetables. Cook, stirring frequently, until golden brown and softened, about 15 minutes.

Add the tomato paste and stir to coat the vegetables. Add the ground lamb and generously season with salt and a small amount of pepper. Using a wooden spoon, delicately mix the meat and vegetables, stirring from the bottom of the pot. Cook until the meat releases its juices, 6 to 8 minutes.

Stir in the wine and cook until the contents of the pan begin to steam. Stir in the *passata*, add the *brodo*, and decrease the heat to low. Cook, stirring occasionally, until the meat is tender, 3 to 5 hours. Begin tasting for tenderness and seasoning after 3 hours.

Transfer 4 cups [900 g] of the ragù to a large high-sided sauté pan or skillet over medium heat. (Store the extra sauce according to the instructions following.) Bring the sauce to a rapid simmer and cook until the the sauce reduces slightly, 3 to 4 minutes. Add the butter and swirl to emulsify. Set the sauce aside.

Bring a large pot of water to a rolling boil over high heat. Season the water with salt (see page 25). When the salt dissolves, add the *garganelli*. Cook until tender, 2½ to 3 minutes.

Meanwhile, return the sauce to medium heat. Using a spider, transfer the pasta to the sauce and stir to coat. Add some pasta cooking water, as needed, to loosen the sauce. Serve immediately with the Pecorino Romano sprinkled on top.

The sauce will keep, refrigerated in an airtight container, for up to 7 days or frozen for up to 6 months.

TRIANG

Triangoli are the first filled pasta I teach my cooks to make and they are where anyone who wants to learn to make fresh filled pasta should start. The process teaches the beginning motions of making slightly more advanced pasta shapes such as Tortelloni (page 148), Balanzoni (page 160), and Tortellini (page 172), while also imparting the supremely important lesson of single thickness (see page 24).

Filled pasta is labor intensive, but you can make it ahead and successfully refrigerate it for about a week, or even freeze it. The key is to blanch the filled pasta first. If you refrigerate *triangoli* or other filled pastas directly after making them, moisture from the filling sweats through the pasta, resulting in a tacky dough. Blanching (see page 136), however, cooks the surface protein of the pasta, which seals the moisture inside the dough and limits the sweating effect.

OLI

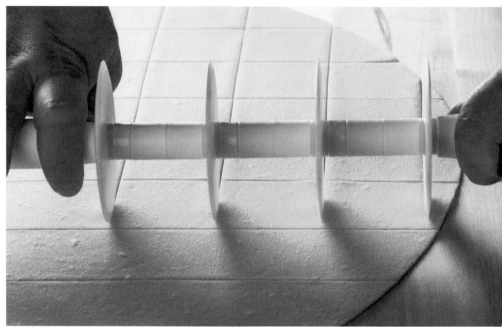

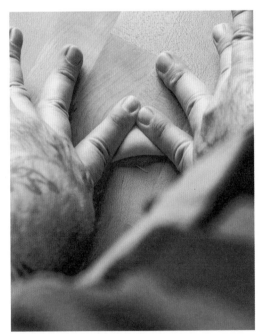

TRIANGOLI

MAKES ABOUT 1.5 KG [53 OZ], INCLUDING FILLING, SERVING 6

1 RECIPE SFOGLIA ALL'UOVO (PAGE 38), AT ROOM TEMPERATURE

1 RECIPE RIPIENO OF CHOICE: RIPIENO DI ZUCCA, RIPIENO DI FORMAGGIO, OR RIPIENO DI RICOTTA (PAGES 138–39)

"00" FLOUR, FOR DUSTING

Roll one dough ball to a thickness of 9 Post-it® Notes on a lightly floured work surface (see page 50). Set it aside on your work surface, uncovered, for 2 to 3 minutes to dry slightly. Cover the *sfoglia* with plastic and let rest for 2 to 3 minutes more.

Set an accordion pastry cutter to 2½ in [6 cm]. Use firm and even pressure to cut the *sfoglia* into strips, moving from south to north. The edge of the pastry cutter should graze the west edge of the *sfoglia*. If the pasta isn't cut all the way through, clean up the rows using a sharp knife. Beginning at the bottom edge of the *sfoglia*, use firm and even pressure to cut the pasta into strips, east to west. Clear away any irregular pieces and add them to your *maltagliati* pile (see page 100).

FILL THE TRIANGOLI: Transfer your *ripieno* of choice to a pastry bag (no tip needed). Cover the pasta with a clean, unscented plastic trash can liner, leaving the first row, closest to you, exposed. Pipe a grape-size amount (about 2 tsp) of filling in the middle of each pasta piece.

SHAPE THE TRIANGOLI: Orient a piece of pasta as a diamond. Using your thumb and index finger, fold the southern tip of the diamond up and over the filling. Join it to the northern tip and seal by pressing the tips together with your thumb and index finger to a single thickness (see page 24). Align your index fingers along the edges of the triangle, forming an inverted "V." Press firmly to seal the entire triangle and create a single thickness.

Transfer the filled pasta to a clean work surface and let dry, uncovered, for 15 minutes. The *triangoli* are ready to use now, or you can blanch them for future use (see sidebar).

Meanwhile, repeat the process with the remaining dough ball and filling.

BLANCHING FILLED PASTA FOR FUTURE USE

Line a work surface with a clean non-terry cloth kitchen towel. Bring a large pot of water to a rolling boil over high heat. Lightly season with salt.

Working in batches to avoid overcrowding, gently drop the filled pasta into the boiling water. As soon as they float, using a spider, transfer to the towel-lined work surface, making sure they are not touching. Repeat with the remaining pasta. If possible, direct a fan on low speed at the pieces to dry them. Turn them every 5 minutes or so until they are completely dry, about 20 minutes with the fan and up to 40 minutes without.

The pasta will keep, refrigerated in an airtight container, for up 10 days or frozen for up to 3 months. When cooking blanched pasta, deduct 15 to 20 seconds from the recommended cooking time. When cooking frozen pasta, cook for 2 minutes longer than the recipe calls for, then begin testing for doneness.

RIPIENO DI ZUCCA

BUTTERNUT SQUASH FILLING

In this recipe you can use any hard winter squash (butternut, acorn, turban, fairytale, Cinderella)—with the exception of spaghetti squash! Note that the filling needs to cool for at least 2 hours before finishing the *triangoli*.

MAKES ABOUT 1 QT [950 G]

ONE 3 LB [1.35 KG] BUTTERNUT SQUASH, PEELED AND CUT INTO 2 IN [5 CM] CUBES

KOSHER SALT

8 TBSP [1 STICK, OR 112 G] UNSALTED BUTTER

2 FRESH SAGE LEAVES

In a medium pot, combine the squash with enough cold water to cover. Bring the water to a boil over high heat and season with salt (see page 25). Cook until the squash is very tender, 20 to 30 minutes. Drain the squash, transfer to the bowl of a food processor, and process until very smooth, about 1 minute.

In a large sauté pan or skillet over medium heat, melt the butter until frothy and golden. Add the sage and cook until fragrant, about 30 seconds. Add the squash and season with salt. Cook, stirring constantly to prevent the filling from sticking to the bottom of the pan, which would caramelize it, until thickened, about 15 minutes. Set the filling aside to cool.

Remove and discard the sage. Transfer the filling to a pastry bag (no tip needed) and refrigerate for at least 2 hours before using.

The filling will keep, refrigerated in the pastry bag (cover the exposed end) or an airtight container, for up to 3 days.

RIPIENO DI RICOTTA

RICOTTA FILLING

You can make your own ricotta (see page 145) for this filling, or buy it.

MAKES ABOUT 1 QT [950 G]

1 LB [454 G] RICOTTA

1 CUP [100 G] FINELY GRATED PARMIGIANO-REGGIANO

1 TSP KOSHER SALT

SCANT TSP FRESHLY GROUND BLACK PEPPER

In a large bowl, combine the ricotta, Parmigiano-Reggiano, salt, and pepper. Whisk vigorously until very smooth, about 1½ minutes. Transfer the ricotta mixture to a pastry bag (no tip needed).

The filling will keep, refrigerated in the pastry bag (cover the exposed end) or an airtight container, for up to 3 days.

RIPIENO DI FORMAGGIO

CHEESE FILLING

This is a classic bolognese pasta filling. Gorgonzola is a blue cheese made in northern Italy. I prefer the *dolce* or "sweet" version of Gorgonzola here; it's milder and softer than its cousin, Gorgonzola *piccante*.

MAKES ABOUT 1 QT [775 G]

4 OZ [113 G] GORGONZOLA DOLCE

8 OZ [227 G] RICOTTA

6 OZ [170 G] MASCARPONE

1½ CUPS [150 G] FINELY GRATED PARMIGIANO-REGGIANO

In the bowl of a food processor, combine the Gorgonzola, ricotta, mascarpone, and Parmigiano-Reggiano and process until smooth, about 2 minutes. Transfer the mixture to a pastry bag (no tip needed).

The filling will keep, refrigerated in the pastry bag (cover the exposed end) or an airtight container, for up to 3 days. Let soften at room temperature for about 15 minutes before using.

Pastry Bags 101

A pastry bag, also called a piping bag, comes in handy for lots of uses (icing cakes and cupcakes, stuffing appetizers, piping perfectly round pancakes) and is the best, easiest, and fastest way to fill pastas. It also lasts a long time and costs just a few dollars, so I recommend getting one. But if you don't have one, a heavy-duty 1 gal [3.8 L] or 1 qt [906 ml] resealable plastic bag will get the job done. Simply fill the bag with ripieno, press out any excess air, seal the bag, and twist the top, gently squeezing to condense the filling into one corner. When you're ready to use the filling, snip off ½ in [12 mm] from that bottom corner. Squeeze from the top, guiding the bag with your dominant hand, as you would a pastry bag. You don't need tips for filling pastas for any of the recipes in this book.

Luciano Occhi, Famed Mattarello and Tagliere Maker

In 2014, Bologna lost one of its greatest artisans. Luciano Occhi, a maestro of carpentry who honed his craft making *mattarelli*—pasta rolling pins—and *taglieri*—pasta boards—passed away at the age of 75. He was one of the last of Italy's artisanal wooden pasta toolmakers. Called Geppetto by some for his ability to practically breathe life into inanimate wood, Luciano had an uncanny ability to craft *mattarelli* that felt like a natural extension of a pasta maker's hands and *taglieri* that brought *sfoglia* to life.

Luciano's genius wasn't just in shaping wood. His job started with choosing the very trees that supplied his workshop. Like a truffle hunter (see page 225), he would track down the ideal tree trunk, from which he would cut planks. Next, he would cure them in an oven for a month at 195°F [90.5°C].

Only when Luciano judged the wood ready to carve was it guided into the calibrator to become a perfectly cylindrical *mattarello*. He also made flawless *taglieri*.

After he passed away, his son Davide Occhi transformed his pre-WWII workshop on Via della Ghisiliera 14 into a kind of museum. Davide lived in Milan at the time and worked for a bank, but devotion to his father's craft, which he learned by his side, eventually led him back to Bologna. At first he would only come down on weekends to finish pieces his father had started. Then he returned permanently to Bologna to continue his father's trade. Artisan *mattarello* making in the city may be reaching its end, but it's not quite there yet.

TRIANGOLI DI ZUCCA CON BURRO E SALVIA

TRIANGOLI WITH PUMPKIN, BUTTER, AND SAGE

In Bologna, you know fall is on its way when squash dishes laced with butter and sage start popping up on menus. Locals eat them with gusto, knowing when squash season is over they will have to wait another six months to enjoy them.

SERVES 6

16 TBSP [2 STICKS, OR 224 G] UNSALTED BUTTER, CUT INTO PIECES

6 TO 8 FRESH SAGE LEAVES

KOSHER SALT

1 RECIPE TRIANGOLI (PAGE 136) FILLED WITH RIPIENO DI ZUCCA (PAGE 138)

1 CUP [100 G] FINELY GRATED PARMIGIANO-REGGIANO

In a large sauté pan or skillet over medium heat, melt the butter until barely frothy. Add the sage and cook just until golden, 15 to 30 seconds. Set the sauce aside.

Bring a large pot of water to a rolling boil over high heat. Season the water with salt (see page 25). When the salt dissolves, add the *triangoli* and cook until tender, 2½ to 3 minutes.

Meanwhile, return the sauce to medium heat. Using a spider, transfer the pasta to the sauce, gently shaking off as much water as possible. Immediately begin swirling the pasta to coat. Serve immediately with the Parmigiano-Reggiano sprinkled on top.

TRIANGOLI AL MIELE CON PECORINO DI FOSSA

TRIANGOLI WITH HONEY AND AGED PECORINO CHEESE

Bologna is Parmigiano-Reggiano's kingdom and this cow's milk cheese is absolutely ubiquitous in the city and its environs. Due to the amount of land devoted to cows, there are few sheep in the area, hence few *pecorini* (sheep's milk cheeses). Pecorino offers a respite from Emilia-Romagna's cow's milk cheese dominance, and one of my favorite types is pecorino *di fossa*, which is cave-aged. I want this salty, creamy, and piquant cheese to really shine here, so it appears both in grated and shaved form. If you can't find it, use any sharp, aged sheep's milk cheese, such as pecorino *sardo* or Pecorino Romano.

SERVES 6

16 TBSP [2 STICKS, OR 224 G] UNSALTED BUTTER, CUT INTO PIECES

KOSHER SALT

1 RECIPE TRIANGOLI (PAGE 136) FILLED WITH RIPIENO DI RICOTTA (PAGE 138) AND 1 TBSP HONEY

½ CUP [50 G] FINELY GRATED PECORINO DI FOSSA OR OTHER PECORINO, PLUS MORE FOR SHAVING

1 TBSP HONEY, FOR DRIZZLING

In a large sauté pan or skillet over high heat, melt the butter. Set the sauce aside.

Bring a large pot of water to a rolling boil over high heat. Season the water with salt (see page 25). When the salt dissolves, add the *triangoli* and cook until tender, 2½ to 3 minutes.

Meanwhile, return the sauce to medium heat. Using a spider, transfer the pasta to the sauce. Add ¼ cup [60 ml] of pasta cooking water and stir to coat. Add the grated pecorino and swirl to incorporate. Serve immediately with honey and more pecorino shaved on top.

Don't Call It Cheese: All About Ricotta

Emilia-Romagna might be one of Italy's wealthiest regions today, but for centuries, many of its residents just barely got by. Nobles benefited from ingredients harvested and foodstuffs crafted by hard-working peasants. Peasants, on the other hand, depended on the nobles' scraps and leftovers for survival—and creatively turned nothing into something. Perhaps the best example of this is ricotta.

First things first: ricotta is not technically a cheese. This creamy substance is not attained through fermentation, so that disqualifies it as *formaggio*. It is, however, the by-product of cheese production. After cheese is made, there is abundant leftover whey. To avoid wasting anything, peasants discovered they could heat the liquid with something acidic—vinegar or lemon juice, for example—and the proteins in the whey would coagulate. They strained these and set them in baskets to form a compact mass. The result was fat- and calorie-rich ricotta (which means "twice cooked"), a culinary godsend the peasants used to enrich simple pasta sauces or enjoyed spread onto bread.

Today, ricotta is sold all over the world, but outside of Italy it's difficult to find versions with the same full, milky flavor and smooth, creamy texture. If the only ricotta readily available to you is commercially produced, the closest approximation to the real deal is then to make your own, which I highly recommend. It is not that difficult. Follow the recipe using the best-quality whole milk you can find; I like Strauss or Clover brands. Don't even think about using skim or ultra-pasteurized milk. If you prefer to purchase ricotta, Bellwether Farms is my favorite domestic producer. And whether you are making or buying ricotta to use in the other recipes in this book, it can be made with any type of milk—from a cow, goat, sheep, or even a buffalo.

RICOTTA

MAKES ABOUT 3 CUPS [750 G]

1 GAL [3.8 L] WHOLE MILK OF CHOICE (SEE HEADNOTE)

1 TBSP KOSHER SALT

½ CUP [120 ML] GOOD RED OR WHITE WINE VINEGAR

Line a fine-mesh strainer or chinois with cheesecloth and set it on a sheet tray or into a large bowl.

In a large heavy-bottomed pot over high heat, heat the milk and salt to 185°F [85°C], about 5 minutes, constantly dragging a rubber spatula across the bottom of the pot in a figure-eight pattern. When the mixture reaches temperature, add the vinegar. Stop stirring and turn off the heat. *Do not touch it or agitate it,* even if it looks like it will boil over (it won't). The liquid will begin to visibly break away from the curds after about 10 minutes. Once this happens, using a fine-mesh spider, transfer the curds to the prepared colander and refrigerate to drain for at least 2 hours.

The ricotta will keep, refrigerated in an airtight container, for up to 4 days.

TRIANGOLI CON GORGONZOLA, RADICCHIO, E ROSMARINO

TRIANGOLI WITH GORGONZOLA, RADICCHIO, AND ROSEMARY

Gorgonzola is often paired with bitter radicchio, creating a beautiful flavor contrast. I like to use Treviso, but you can use any type of radicchio you wish, or even substitute escarole, dandelion greens, or chicory.

SERVES 6

4 TBSP [56 G] UNSALTED BUTTER

2 SPRIGS ROSEMARY

½ MEDIUM HEAD RADICCHIO, CUT INTO BITE-SIZE PIECES

KOSHER SALT

FRESHLY GROUND BLACK PEPPER

1 RECIPE TRIANGOLI (PAGE 136) FILLED WITH RIPIENO DI FORMAGGIO (PAGE 139)

½ CUP [50 G] FINELY GRATED PARMIGIANO-REGGIANO

In a large sauté pan or skillet over medium-high heat, melt the butter until frothy and golden. Add the rosemary and cook until fragrant, about 15 seconds. Add the radicchio and season with salt and pepper. Cook, tossing and stirring, until the leaves are wilted, about 2 minutes. Set the sauce aside.

Bring a large pot of water to a rolling boil over high heat. Season the water with salt (see page 25). When the salt dissolves, add the *triangoli* and cook until tender, 2½ to 3 minutes.

Meanwhile, return the sauce to medium heat. Using a spider, transfer the pasta to the sauce and swirl to coat. Add some pasta cooking water, as needed, to loosen the sauce. Serve immediately with the Parmigiano-Reggiano sprinkled on top.

TORTEL

I have eaten my body weight in *tortelloni* (think: very big tortellini filled with a ricotta mixture instead of ground pork). Let's say it's all been in the name of research. The variance of shapes, textures, and thickness I have encountered is mind boggling, particularly considering the fact that *tortelloni* are, at least superficially, pinched pasta parcels. The way the pasta is folded, however, makes it unique to the pasta maker and, for that reason, there are as many *tortelloni* shapes as there are *sfoglini* in Bologna.

I firmly believe the only way to make a proper *tortellone* is to think about its architecture. When cooked, most *tortelloni* will have thick and crunchy parts or chewy parts. That's because there are many connection points created through folding where the pasta is at double or even quadruple thickness at the folds, resulting in uneven cooking. By folding a *tortellone* my way and pressing the pasta to single thickness (see page 24) at the connection points, you create channels for the boiling water to flow through and, thereby, ensure even cooking.

LONI

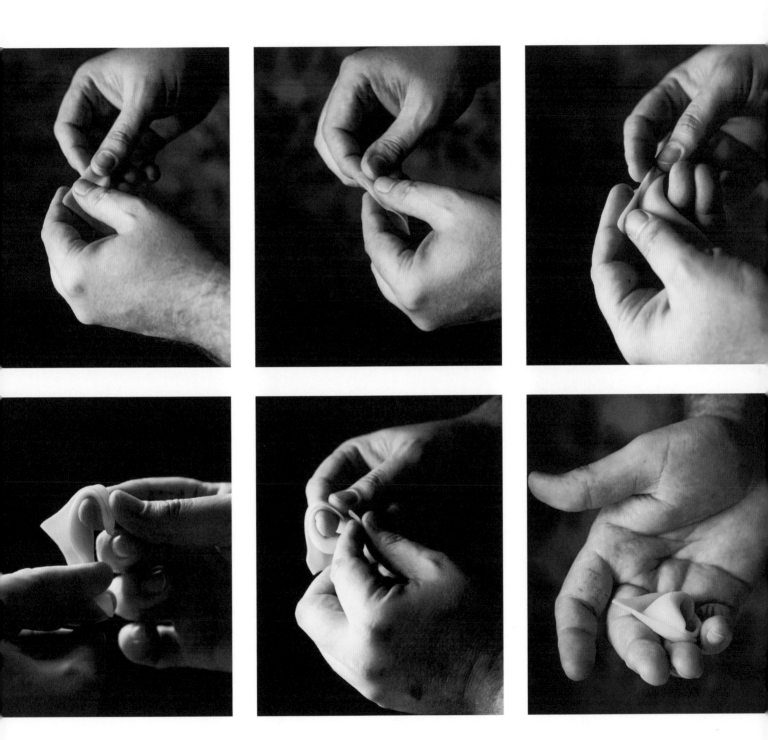

TORTELLONI

MAKES ABOUT 1.7 KG [60 OZ], INCLUDING FILLING, SERVING 6

1 RECIPE SFOGLIA ALL'UOVO (PAGE 38), AT ROOM TEMPERATURE

"00" FLOUR, FOR DUSTING

2 LB [908 G] RICOTTA

1 CUP PLUS 2 TBSP [112.5 G] FINELY GRATED PARMIGIANO-REGGIANO

1 TSP KOSHER SALT

1 EXTRA-LARGE EGG

3 TBSP CHOPPED FRESH FLAT-LEAF PARSLEY

Roll one dough ball to a thickness of 9 Post-it® Notes on a lightly floured work surface (see page 50). Set it aside on your work surface, uncovered, for 2 to 3 minutes to dry slightly. Cover the *sfoglia* with plastic and let rest for 2 to 3 minutes more.

Set an accordion pastry cutter to 2½ in [6 cm]. Use firm and even pressure to cut the *sfoglia* into strips, moving from south to north. The edge of the pastry cutter should graze the west edge of the *sfoglia*. Beginning at the bottom edge of the *sfoglia*, use firm and even pressure to cut the *sfoglia* into strips, east to west. Clear away any irregular pieces and add them to your *maltagliati* pile (see page 100). Cover the *sfoglia* with a clean, unscented plastic trash can liner, leaving the first row, closest to you, exposed.

MAKE THE FILLING: In a large bowl, combine the ricotta, Parmigiano-Reggiano, salt, and the egg. Whisk vigorously until very smooth, about 1½ minutes. Using a spatula, fold in the parsley. Transfer the ricotta mixture to a pastry bag (no tip needed).

The filling will keep, refrigerated in the pastry bag (cover the exposed end) or an airtight container, for up to 3 days.

FILL THE TORTELLONI: Pipe a grape-size amount (about 2 tsp) of *ripieno* in the middle of each pasta piece.

SHAPE THE TORTELLONI: Orient a piece of pasta as a diamond in the palm of one hand. Using your thumb and index finger, fold the southern tip of the diamond up and over the filling. Join it to the northern tip, forming a triangle. Using those same two fingers, seal the triangle just at the top, pressing the pasta to a single thickness (see page 24).

With the same hand, use your thumb and index finger to connect and seal one edge of the triangle. Transfer the pasta to your opposite hand and seal the remaining edge of the triangle.

Transfer the sealed triangle back to your other hand, gripping it with your index finger and thumb at the pressed tip. To make the fold, support the bottom of the filling with a hooked index finger. Then, with your thumb, fold the sealed flap toward you, gently forming a crease on that side while running your thumb from the top of the triangle down toward the tip. Once at the tip, grip the crease delicately with your thumb and hooked index finger and allow it to hang.

Repeat on the other side and, in one motion, wrap the pasta around your index finger and connect the two tips, pressing the connection points to a single thickness (see page 24).

As each *tortellone* is shaped, place it on a clean work surface, taking care not to let it touch the other pieces. Repeat the filling and shaping with the remaining dough, working one row at a time. Allow the shaped pasta to dry on your work surface, uncovered, for about 15 minutes. The *tortelloni* are ready to use now, or you can blanch them for future use (see page 136).

Meanwhile, repeat the process with the remaining dough ball and filling.

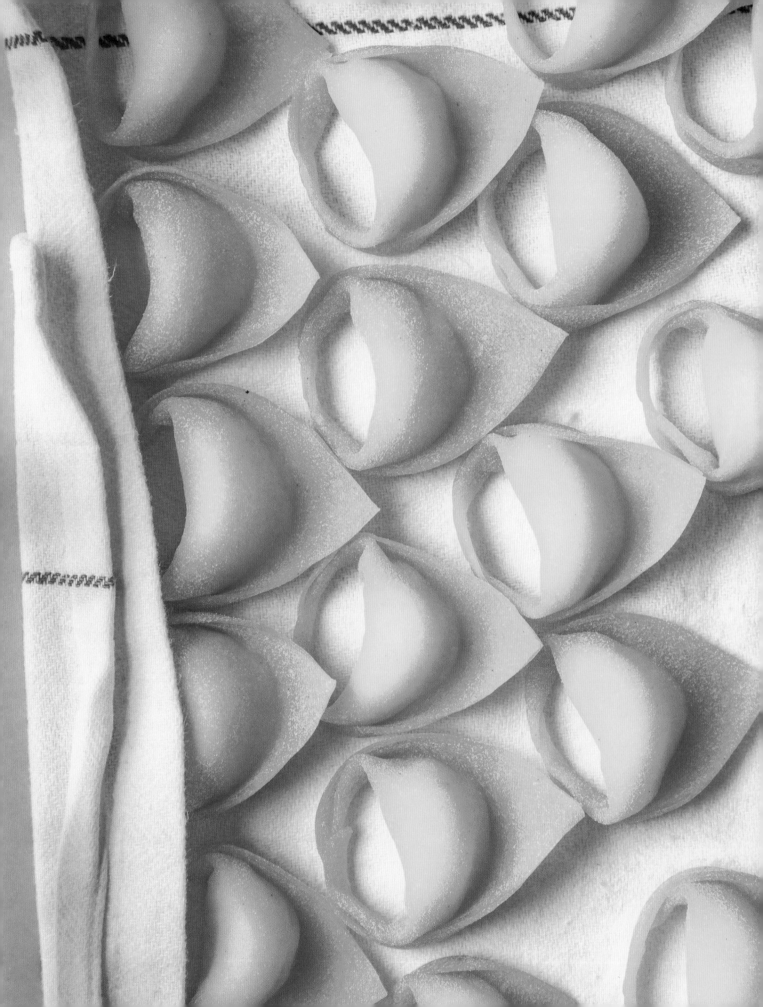

TORTELLONI BURRO E ORO

TORTELLONI WITH BUTTER AND TOMATO

Tomatoes may be synonymous with Italian cuisine, but they are mostly conspicuously absent from the cuisine of Bologna. The local custom calls for tomatoes to be harvested in summer when extended families get together, then blanched, milled, and bottled, or even just blanched, skinned, and bottled whole. These products are then used sparingly throughout the coming year, hence the association with *oro* (gold) in the recipe title.

In classic bolognese style, the tomatoes here aren't flavored with olive oil or garlic or basil—just a big old knob of butter, which imparts a rich, velvety elegance that clings beautifully to the pasta.

SERVES 6

3 CUPS [675 G] PASSATA DI POMODORO (PAGE 236)

16 TBSP [2 STICKS, OR 224 G] UNSALTED BUTTER, CUT INTO PIECES

KOSHER SALT

1 RECIPE TORTELLONI (PAGE 152)

1 CUP [100 G] FINELY GRATED PARMIGIANO-REGGIANO

In a large sauté pan or skillet over medium heat, bring the *passata* to a rapid simmer. Add the butter, season with salt, and swirl to emulsify, about 90 seconds. Set the sauce aside.

Bring a large pot of water to a rolling boil over high heat. Season the water with salt (see page 25). When the salt dissolves, add the *tortelloni* and cook until very tender, 2½ to 3 minutes.

Meanwhile, return the sauce to medium heat. Using a spider, transfer the pasta to the sauce and gently swirl to coat. Add some pasta cooking water, as needed, to loosen the sauce. Add 2 Tbsp of Parmigiano-Reggiano and swirl to incorporate. Serve immediately with the remaining Parmigiano-Reggiano sprinkled on top.

TORTELLONI CON RAGÙ BIANCO DI MAIALE

TORTELLONI WITH PORK RAGÙ

It's a common misconception that all meat ragùs have tomato sauce in them. This "white" ragù is proof you don't miss anything by omitting it. On the contrary, the absence of the tomato's acid lets the lovely porkiness of the dish shine through unadulterated. You can use the sauce right away, but I think it's improved after sitting in the refrigerator overnight, or for up to 3 days. Just be sure to let it cool completely before refrigerating and keep it tightly covered. If you don't have a meat grinder, ask your butcher to grind the meat for you. Use any leftover sauce to dress pasta for another meal, or eat smeared on bread.

SERVES 6; MAKES 3 QT/12 CUPS [2.4 KG] SAUCE

2 LB [907 G] BONELESS PORK SHOULDER, CUT INTO ½ IN [12 MM] CUBES

5 OZ [141 G] PANCETTA, CUT INTO ½ IN [12 MM] CUBES

5 OZ [141 G] PROSCIUTTO DI PARMA, CUT INTO ½ IN [12 MM] CUBES

5 OZ [141 G] MORTADELLA, CUT INTO ½ IN [12 MM] CUBES

4 CELERY STALKS, ROUGHLY CHOPPED

1 LARGE YELLOW ONION, ROUGHLY CHOPPED

1 LARGE CARROT, ROUGHLY CHOPPED

5 OZ [141 G] STRUTTO

KOSHER SALT

FRESHLY GROUND BLACK PEPPER

2 CUPS [480 ML] DRY WHITE WINE

3 CUPS [709 ML] BRODO DI CARNE (PAGE 237), OR LOW-SODIUM CHICKEN BROTH

2 TBSP UNSALTED BUTTER

1 RECIPE TORTELLONI (PAGE 152)

1 CUP [100 G] FINELY GRATED PARMIGIANO-REGGIANO

Using a meat grinder, or a grinder attachment, fitted with a large die, grind the pork shoulder into a large bowl and set aside. Without cleaning the grinder, grind the pancetta and prosciutto two times into a medium bowl. Grind the mortadella into the same medium bowl and set aside. Grind the celery, onion, and carrot into another medium bowl and set aside.

In a large heavy-bottomed pot over medium-high heat, melt the *strutto*. Add the ground pancetta, prosciutto, and mortadella and cook until the fat from the pancetta has rendered, about 4 minutes. Add the ground vegetables and cook, stirring frequently, until they are golden and tender, around 15 minutes.

Add the ground pork and generously season with salt and a small amount of pepper. Using a wooden spoon, gently mix the meat and vegetables, stirring from the bottom of the pot. Cook until the meat releases its juices, 4 to 6 minutes. Stir in the wine and cook until the contents of the pan begin to steam. Stir in the *brodo* and turn the heat to low.

Cook, uncovered, stirring occasionally, until the meat is tender, 3 to 5 hours. Begin tasting for fork-tenderness and seasoning after 3 hours. Transfer 4 cups [1 kg] of sauce to a large sauté pan or skillet over medium heat. (Store the extra sauce according to the instructions following.) Bring the sauce to a rapid simmer and cook until the sauce reduces slightly, about 2 minutes. Add the butter and swirl to emulsify. Set the sauce aside.

Bring a large pot of water to a rolling boil over high heat. Season the water with salt (see page 25). When the salt dissolves, add the *tortelloni* and cook until very tender, 2½ to 3 minutes.

Meanwhile, return the sauce to medium heat. Using a spider, transfer the pasta to the sauce and stir to coat. Add some pasta cooking water, as needed, to loosen the sauce. Serve immediately with the Parmigiano-Reggiano sprinkled on top.

The sauce will keep, refrigerated in an airtight container, for up to 10 days or frozen for up to 6 months.

TORTELLONI CON SPECK E NOCI

TORTELLONI WITH SMOKED HAM AND WALNUTS

The combination of walnuts and *speck*–a smoked cured ham from Italy's Alto Adige region, which shares a border with Austria–is popular all over the northern part of the country. But despite Bologna's deep pride in its own regional foods, delicious things from the north (especially porky ones) are known to make their way into local kitchens. This dish is a good example of that. You might even say the spiced and smoky *speck* provides a savory breather from prosciutto di Parma, the sweet, ubiquitous cured ham from Emilia-Romagna. If you can't get your hands on *speck*, substitute thinly sliced Virginia country ham.

SERVES 6

2 CUPS [240 G] WALNUT HALVES

16 TBSP [2 STICKS, OR 224 G] UNSALTED BUTTER, CUT INTO PIECES

4 OZ [113.5 G] SPECK, THINLY SLICED AND TORN INTO SLIGHTLY LARGER THAN BITE-SIZE PIECES

6 FRESH SAGE LEAVES, TORN

KOSHER SALT

1 RECIPE TORTELLONI (PAGE 152)

1 CUP [100 G] FINELY GRATED PARMIGIANO-REGGIANO

Preheat the oven to 300°F [150°C]. Line a baking sheet with parchment paper.

Spread the walnuts evenly over the prepared baking sheet and toast in the oven until mahogany colored, about 10 minutes. Transfer to the bowl of a food processor and pulse until the walnuts are the size of peas, about 1 minute. Alternatively, once they are cool enough to handle, transfer them to a cutting board and chop with a chef's knife.

In a large sauté pan or skillet over medium heat, melt the butter until frothy and golden. Add the speck and cook until browned, about 30 seconds. Add the walnuts and sage and cook until fragrant, about 30 seconds. Set the sauce aside.

Bring a large pot of water to a rolling boil over high heat. Season the water with salt (see page 25). When the salt dissolves, add the *tortelloni* and cook until tender, 2½ to 3 minutes.

Meanwhile, return the sauce to medium heat. Using a spider, transfer the pasta to the sauce and stir to coat. Add some pasta cooking water, as needed, to loosen the sauce. Serve immediately with the Parmigiano-Reggiano sprinkled on top.

BALANZ

February in Bologna is tough. By the beginning of the month the city is already four solid months into frosty weather, and overcast days far outnumber those filled with sunshine. For this—and the obvious Catholic—reason, the city really looks forward to *Carnevale*. The dishes prepared for this holiday are even richer and more elaborate than Bologna's everyday cooking. Among these, *balanzoni* are named for a famous doctor, a studious Renaissance man whose wealth of knowledge is represented by the mixture of pasta fillings—mascarpone, mortadella, ricotta, and herbs.

Dr. Balanzoni's namesake pasta is, essentially, slightly larger *tortelloni* made with Sfoglia Verde agli Spinaci (page 42). *Balanzoni* are the third largest of the four *tortello* shapes: tortellini being the smallest, *tortelloni* next smallest, and *tortellaccio*—not covered here—the largest.

Due to the Spinach Dough, which interferes with the gluten development, *balanzoni* are less delicate than tortellini or *tortelloni*. They also require a longer cooking time because the dough isn't rolled as thinly.

ONI

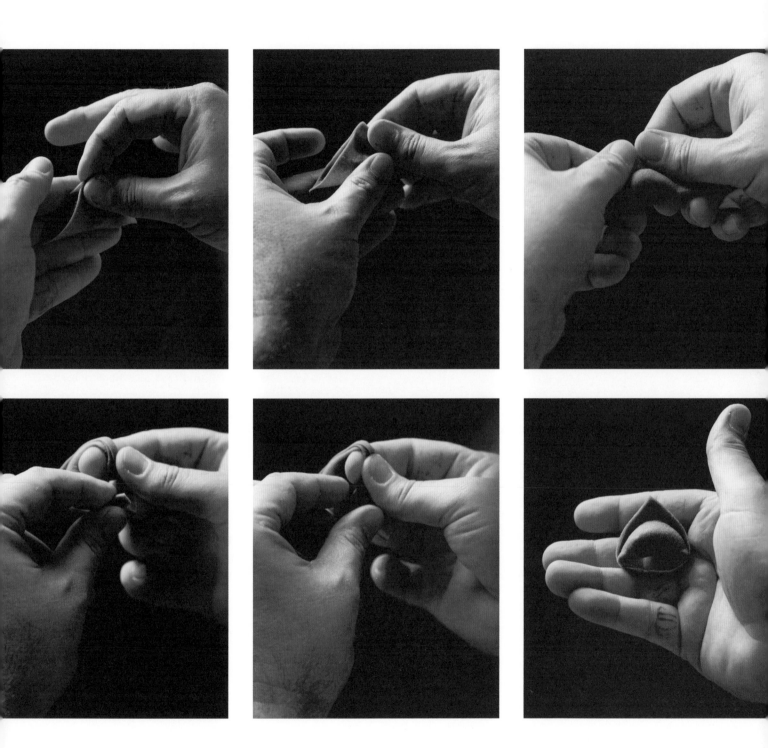

BALANZONI

MAKES ABOUT 1.9 KG [67 OZ], INCLUDING FILLING, SERVING 6

1 RECIPE SFOGLIA VERDE AGLI SPINACI (PAGE 42), AT ROOM TEMPERATURE

"00" FLOUR, FOR DUSTING

1½ LB [681 G] MORTADELLA, CUT INTO 1 IN [2.5 CM] CUBES

12 OZ [340 G] RICOTTA

4 OZ [113.5 G] MASCARPONE

½ CUP [50 G] FINELY GRATED PARMIGIANO-REGGIANO

2 TBSP CHOPPED FRESH FLAT-LEAF PARSLEY

Roll one dough ball to a thickness of 9 Post-it® Notes on a lightly floured work surface (see page 50). Set it aside on your work surface, uncovered, for 2 to 3 minutes to dry slightly. Cover the *sfoglia* with plastic and let rest for 2 to 3 minutes more.

Set an accordion pastry cutter to 3 in [7.5 cm]. Use firm and even pressure to cut the *sfoglia* into strips, moving from south to north. The edge of the pastry cutter should graze the west edge of the *sfoglia*. Beginning at the bottom edge of the *sfoglia*, use firm and even pressure to cut the *sfoglia* into strips, east to west. Clear away any irregular pieces and add them to your *maltagliati* pile (see page 100). Cover the *sfoglia* with a clean, unscented plastic trash can liner, leaving the first row, closest to you, exposed.

MAKE THE FILLING: Using a meat grinder, or a grinder attachment, fitted with a medium die, grind the mortadella two times into a large bowl. Add the ricotta, mascarpone, and Parmigiano-Reggiano. Using a rubber spatula, fold the ingredients together until very smooth, about 1 minute. Fold in the parsley. Transfer the filling to a pastry bag (no tip needed).

The filling will keep, refrigerated in the pastry bag (cover the exposed end) or an airtight container, for up to 3 days. Use at room temperature.

FILL THE BALANZONI: Pipe a chestnut-size amount (about 1 Tbsp) of *ripieno* in the middle of each pasta piece.

SHAPE THE BALANZONI: Orient a piece of pasta as a diamond in the palm of one hand. Using your thumb and index finger, fold the southern tip of the diamond up and over the filling. Join it to the northern tip, forming a triangle. Using those same two fingers, seal the triangle just at the top, pressing the pasta to a single thickness (see page 24).

With the same hand, use your thumb and index finger to connect and seal one edge of the triangle. Transfer the pasta to your opposite hand, and seal the remaining edge of the triangle.

Transfer the sealed triangle back to your other hand, gripping it with your index finger and thumb at the pressed tip. To make the fold, support the bottom of the filling with a hooked index and middle finger. With your thumb, fold the sealed flap toward you, gently forming a crease on that side while running your thumb from the top of the triangle down toward the tip. Once at the tip, delicately grip the crease with your thumb and hooked index and middle finger and allow it to hang.

Repeat on the other side and, in one motion, wrap the pasta around your index finger and connect the two tips, pressing the connection points into a single thickness (see page 24).

As each *balanzone* is shaped, place it on a clean work surface, taking care not to let it touch the other pieces. Repeat filling and shaping with the remaining dough pieces, working one row at a time. Allow the shaped pasta to dry, uncovered, on your work surface for about 15 minutes. The *balanzoni* are ready to use now, or you can blanch them for future use (see page 136).

Meanwhile, repeat the process with the remaining dough ball and filling.

BALANZONI CON BURRO FUSO E AROMI MISTI

BALANZONI WITH BUTTER, HERBS, AND SPICES

The first time I saw this dish, I was put off–the buttery sauce was a mess of woody sprigs, a veritable minefield of nature. Until that point I had spent most of my career meticulously picking the leaves off herb stems and hadn't yet experienced the low-key approach of tossing entire sprigs into a pan, frying them in butter, and tossing the perfumed lot onto a finished dish. As I've since learned, the result is unbelievably flavorful and the process unimaginably liberating.

SERVES 6

16 TBSP [2 STICKS, OR 224 G] UNSALTED BUTTER, CUT INTO PIECES

4 WHOLE CLOVES

ONE 2 IN [5 CM] CINNAMON STICK, BROKEN IN HALF

1 SPRIG ROSEMARY

1 SPRIG THYME

1 SPRIG MARJORAM

1 FRESH BAY LEAF, TORN, OR 1 DRIED BAY LEAF, WHOLE

4 FRESH SAGE LEAVES, TORN

10 FRESH MINT LEAVES, TORN

4 FRESH BASIL LEAVES, TORN

SCANT TSP FENNEL POLLEN (OPTIONAL)

SMALL PINCH OF NUTMEG, PREFERABLY FRESHLY GRATED

KOSHER SALT

1 RECIPE BALANZONI (PAGE 164)

1 CUP [100 G] FINELY GRATED PARMIGIANO-REGGIANO

In a large sauté pan or skillet over medium heat, melt the butter until frothy and golden. Add the cloves, cinnamon stick, rosemary, thyme, marjoram, bay leaf, and sage and cook until fragrant, about 10 seconds. Add the mint, basil, fennel pollen (if using), and nutmeg and swirl for 5 to 10 seconds to combine. Set the sauce aside.

Bring a large pot of water to a rolling boil over high heat. Season the water with salt (see page 25). When the salt dissolves, add the *balanzoni* and cook until tender, 2½ to 3 minutes.

Return the sauce to medium heat. Using a spider, transfer the pasta to the sauce, gently shaking off as much water as possible. Immediately begin swirling the pasta to coat. Serve immediately with the Parmigiano-Reggiano sprinkled on top.

BALANZONI BURRO E NOCCIOLE

BALANZONI WITH BUTTER AND HAZELNUTS

To get the rich, round flavor I desire from the hazelnuts in this recipe, I slowly cook them in butter on the stovetop. Starting the nuts in a cold pan and heating them with the fat gently releases their warm, delicately astringent flavor and slightly sweet aroma. It's much more effective than toasting.

SERVES 6

16 TBSP [2 STICKS, OR 224 G] UNSALTED BUTTER, CUT INTO PIECES

KOSHER SALT

6 TO 8 FRESH SAGE LEAVES

1½ CUP [180 G] HAZELNUTS, ROUGHLY CHOPPED

1 RECIPE BALANZONI (PAGE 164)

1 CUP [100 G] FINELY GRATED PARMIGIANO-REGGIANO

In a large sauté pan or skillet combine the butter, salt, sage, and hazelnuts. Place the skillet over medium heat and cook until the hazelnuts just begin to color, about 4 minutes. Set the sauce aside.

Bring a large pot of water to a rolling boil over high heat. Season the water with salt (see page 25). When the salt dissolves, add the *balanzoni* and cook until tender, 2½ to 3 minutes.

Return the sauce to medium heat. Using a spider, transfer the pasta to the sauce, gently shaking off as much water as possible. Immediately begin swirling the pasta to coat. Serve immediately with the Parmigiano-Reggiano sprinkled on top.

BALANZONI CON SALSICCIA, PANNA, E SALVIA

BALANZONI WITH SAUSAGE, CREAM, AND SAGE

The festive nature of *balanzoni* is very much in line with the indulgent sauces with which they are generally paired. Here, the soft, round flavors of the pasta filling mingle seductively with the creamy, herbaceous, sausage-studded sauce. Use Italian sausage made without fennel, as it could overpower the sage.

SERVES 6

2 TBSP UNSALTED BUTTER

4 SWEET ITALIAN SAUSAGES (ABOUT 1 LB [454 G] TOTAL), CASINGS REMOVED

6 FRESH SAGE LEAVES

1.5 CUPS [360 ML] HEAVY CREAM

KOSHER SALT

1 RECIPE BALANZONI (PAGE 164)

1 CUP [100 G] FINELY GRATED PARMIGIANO-REGGIANO

In a large sauté pan or skillet over medium-high heat, melt the butter until frothy and golden. Add the sausage and cook, breaking it up with the back of a wooden spoon, until browned, 2 to 3 minutes. Add the sage and cook until very fragrant, about 30 seconds. Add the cream and simmer until reduced by half, about 3 minutes. Set the sauce aside.

Bring a large pot of water to a rolling boil over high heat. Season the water with salt (see page 25). When the salt dissolves, add the *balanzoni* and cook until tender, 2½ to 3 minutes.

Meanwhile, return the sauce to medium heat. Using a spider, transfer the pasta to the sauce, gently shaking off as much water as possible. Immediately begin swirling the pasta to coat. Add ¼ cup [25 g] of Parmigiano-Reggiano and continue to swirl gently until incorporated, adding some pasta cooking water, as needed, to loosen the sauce. Serve immediately with the remaining Parmigiano-Reggiano sprinkled on top.

TORTEL

The first time I ate the *maestra*'s tortellini, back in 2007, it was actually the first time I had ever eaten tortellini—period. I'm not the first chef to have his life changed with a single dish, but the experience of eating tortellini *in brodo* was more than just a life-altering moment. I had never had anything with such a round, full, balanced flavor. The pasta, filling, and broth were all in perfect harmony and I have been chasing that equilibrium in my own food—and that of others—ever since. That defining moment set the benchmark so high, I'm still chasing that level of perfection.

Tortellini tastes of a time and a place. Perfection is achieved through the simplicity and balance of ingredients and from their traditional assembly. Pasta is kneaded and rolled as it has been for centuries. Filling is crafted to complement the flavor and pliability of the pasta. But where did Bologna's most famous pasta (tied with tagliatelle) come from?

Any pasta shape that has made it through Italy's massive cultural shifts of the twentieth century into modern times has a certain amount of lore connected to it. The story I heard about tortellini is an old medieval one, a tale of Jupiter and Venus. The two gods were fighting a great battle on Earth, which wore them out. They took a break to feast and sleep at a nearby inn. Struck by the sheer beauty of these two deities, the innkeeper couldn't help but peek through the keyhole of their door to observe them in their room—that's when he saw Venus's navel, the most beautiful navel he had ever seen. So inspired was he by that seductive navel, he rushed to the kitchen to create something that reflected his new obsession: that something was tortellini. Look at a *tortellino* upside down and you can see a belly and a navel.

The divine creation of tortellini demonstrates its place in Bologna's consciousness (if not necessarily its true origin). And, what we do know for sure is, every single *tortellino* is a fingerprint of its maker. The process is repetitive and, after

LINI

you've done it enough times, each piece will be uniform and completely distinct to the pasta maker.

Once you learn the technique, size is the hardest part to improve upon. My tortellini are considered massive by bolognese standards, but I think they're the right size for American palates. In Italy, a good *sfoglino* will show their prowess by making excessively small tortellini. I have huge fingers, so I can't make the super, super tiny ones. Your tortellini will have your personal signature.

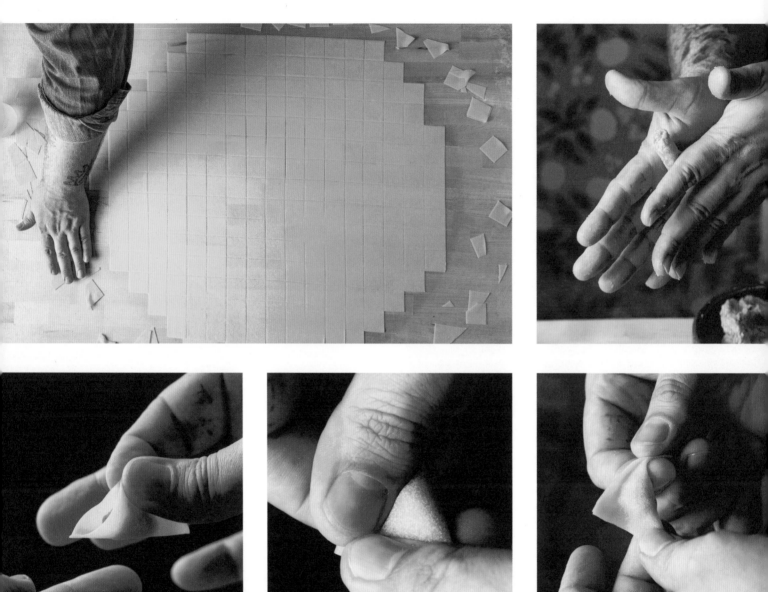

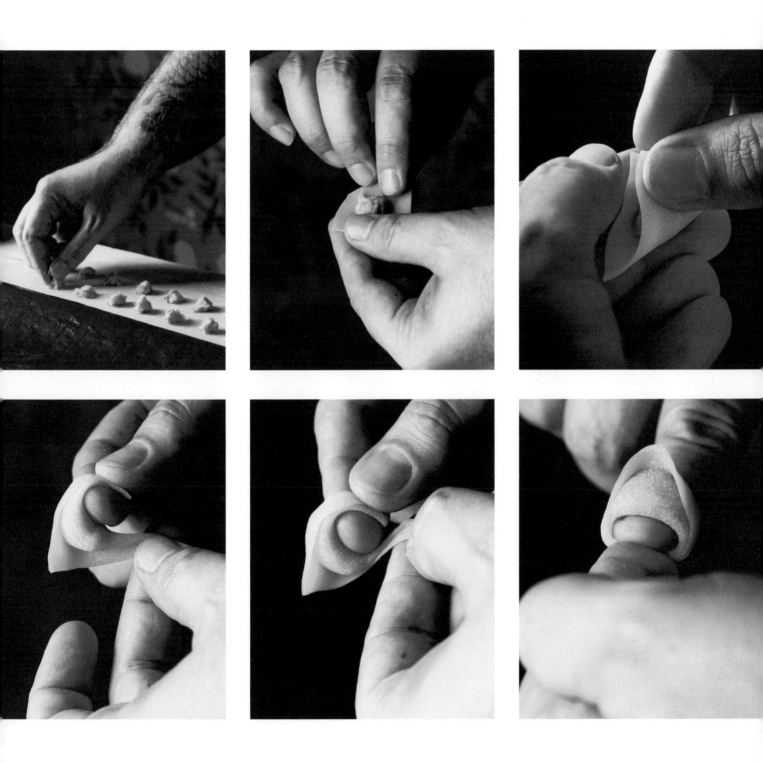

TORTELLINI

MAKES ABOUT 1.5 KG [53 OZ],
SERVING 6

1 RECIPE SFOGLIA ALL'UOVO (PAGE 38),
AT ROOM TEMPERATURE

"00" FLOUR, FOR DUSTING

28 OZ [795 G] RIPIENO DI TORTELLINI
(PAGE 178)

Roll one dough ball to a thickness of 4 Post-it® Notes on a lightly floured work surface (see page 50) and begin cutting immediately. Set an accordion pastry cutter to 1¼ in [3 cm]. Use firm and even pressure to cut the *sfoglia* into strips, moving from south to north. The edge of the pastry cutter should graze the west edge of the *sfoglia*. Beginning at the bottom edge of the *sfoglia*, use firm and even pressure to cut the *sfoglia* into strips, east to west. Clear away any irregular pieces and add them to your *maltagliati* pile (see page 100).

FILL THE TORTELLINI: Take a handful of *ripieno*, about the size of a ping-pong ball (about 3 Tbsp) and roll it into a snake about the thickness of a pencil and the length of your palm. Set aside any excess. Pinch off a piece of filling about the size of a pea and dab it in the center of a pasta square. Repeat until all the pasta squares have dabs of filling on them. Cover the *sfoglia* with a clean, unscented plastic trash can liner, leaving a single row exposed.

SHAPE THE TORTELLINI: Pick up a piece of pasta by the filling—not by the dough itself. Orient the pasta as a diamond on the index and middle finger of one hand. Using your other thumb and index finger, fold the southern tip of the diamond up and over the filling. Join it to the northern tip, forming a triangle. Using those same two fingers, seal the triangle, just at the top, pressing the pasta to a single thickness (see page 24).

With the same hand, use your thumb and index finger to connect and seal one edge of the triangle. Transfer the pasta to your other index and middle fingers and use the other hand to seal the remaining edge of the triangle.

Transfer the sealed triangle back to your other hand, gripping it with your index finger and thumb at the pressed tip. To make the fold, support the bottom of the filling with a hooked index finger. With your thumb, fold the sealed flap toward you, gently forming a crease on that side while running your thumb from the top of the triangle down toward the tip. Once at the tip, grip the crease delicately with your thumb and hooked index finger and allow it to hang.

Repeat on the other side and, in one motion, wrap the pasta around your index finger and connect the two tips, pressing the connection points to a single thickness (see page 24).

As each *tortellino* is shaped, place it on a clean work surface, taking care not to let it touch the other pieces. Repeat filling and shaping the remaining dough, working one row at a time. Allow the shaped pasta to dry, uncovered, on your work surface for about 15 minutes. The tortellini are ready to use now, or you can blanch them for future use (see page 136).

Meanwhile, repeat the process with the remaining dough ball and filling.

RIPIENO DI TORTELLINI

TORTELLINI FILLING

The traditional filling for tortellini is composed of the *fiori di Emilia*—the flowers—or prized ingredients of Emilia-Romagna: Parmigiano-Reggiano, the undisputed king of cheeses; prosciutto di Parma, the prized cured ham from Parma; and mortadella, the apex of sausage making in Bologna. The mixture is further seasoned with wine and bound with egg.

Each filling is unique to a family and, while the essential *fiori* never change, some might add chicken, veal, or other cuts to the mix. My recipe is that of the Spisni family, a humble mixture that Alessandra's great-grandparents would have known.

At the deli counter, ask for the charcuterie to be sliced at least a finger's width. That way you can cube it and grind it more easily. In Bologna, they don't use mortadella with pistachios. If you can't find mortadella without them, pick out the nuts before you grind it. Finally, there is no way around not having a grinder for this recipe. A simple attachment for a KitchenAid™ is best.

This recipe makes enough filling for a double batch of Tortellini (page 176). However, you can freeze the filling for up 6 months. You can also spread it on pieces of bread, toss it with pasta and butter, or fold it into scrambled eggs. It's delicious that way, too. Or, use it for Smeraldine alla Panna (page 184) if you aren't up for making a batch of that pasta's filling, which is similar.

MAKES ABOUT 2½ LB [1.1 KG] FILLING, OR 2 BATCHES

8 OZ [227 G] BONELESS PORK SHOULDER

1 SCANT TBSP KOSHER SALT

1 TSP FRESHLY GROUND BLACK PEPPER

4 TBSP [56 G] UNSALTED BUTTER

½ CUP [120 ML] DRY WHITE WINE

12 OZ [340 G] PROSCIUTTO DI PARMA, CUT INTO ½ IN [12 MM] CUBES

8 OZ [227 G] MORTADELLA WITHOUT PISTACHIOS, CUT INTO ½ IN [12 MM] CUBES

1 LARGE EGG

¾ CUP [75 G] FINELY GRATED PARMIGIANO-REGGIANO

2 SMALL PINCHES OF NUTMEG, PREFERABLY FRESHLY GRATED

Season the pork shoulder with the salt and pepper and set it aside on a tray. In a medium sauté pan or skillet over medium-high heat, melt the butter until frothy and golden. Decrease the heat to medium and add the pork shoulder. Sear until golden on all sides, basting frequently with the hot butter, about 4 minutes each side. Be careful not to burn the butter.

Add the wine and cover the pan. Decrease the heat to low and cook for 5 minutes, turning the pork once halfway through the cooking time. Transfer the pork and any liquid to a large bowl and set aside to cool for about 10 minutes. Cut the pork into ½ in [12 mm] cubes, reserving the liquid.

Using a meat grinder, or a grinder attachment, fitted with a medium die, grind the prosciutto two times into a large bowl. Without cleaning the grinder, grind the mortadella and pork shoulder into the same bowl. Add the egg, Parmigiano-Reggiano, reserved liquid, and nutmeg to the meat mixture. Knead the filling until smooth.

The filling will keep, refrigerated in an airtight container, for up to 10 days or frozen for up to 6 months.

RIPIENO PER SMERALDINE

SMERALDINE FILLING

For this recipe, Maestra Alessandra tweaks her classic tortellini filling (see facing page) slightly to create a softer texture, which she (correctly) claims is a better match for the cream sauce the *smeraldine* (see page 184) are served with.

**MAKES ABOUT 2½ LB [1.1 KG] FILLING,
FOR AROUND 400 SMERALDINE,
OR 2 BATCHES**

8 OZ [227 G] BONELESS PORK SHOULDER

1 SCANT TSP KOSHER SALT

1 SCANT TSP FRESHLY GROUND BLACK PEPPER

4 TBSP [56 G] UNSALTED BUTTER

½ CUP [120 ML] DRY WHITE WINE

**12 OZ [340 G] PROSCUITTO DI PARMA,
CUT INTO ½ IN [12 MM] CUBES**

**1 (ABOUT 4 OZ (113 G]) SWEET ITALIAN
SAUSAGE WITHOUT FENNEL, CASINGS REMOVED**

**4 OZ [113.5 G] MORTADELLA WITHOUT PISTACHIOS,
CUT INTO ½ IN [12 MM] CUBES**

1 LARGE EGG

**1 CUP [100 G] FINELY GRATED
PARMIGIANO-REGGIANO**

**SMALL PINCH OF NUTMEG,
PREFERABLY FRESHLY GRATED**

Generously season the pork shoulder with the salt and pepper and set it aside on a tray. In a medium sauté pan or skillet over medium-high heat, melt the butter until frothy and golden. Turn the heat to medium and add the pork shoulder. Sear until golden on all sides, basting frequently with the hot butter, about 4 minutes total. Be careful not to burn the butter.

Add the wine and cover the pan. Turn the heat to low and cook for 5 minutes, turning the pork once halfway through the cooking time. Transfer the pork and any liquid to a large bowl and set aside to cool for about 10 minutes. Cut the pork shoulder into ½ in [12 mm] cubes, reserving the liquid.

Using a meat grinder, or a grinder attachment, fitted with a medium die, grind the prosciutto two times into a large bowl. Without cleaning the grinder, grind the sausage, mortadella, and pork shoulder into the same bowl. Add the egg, Parmigiano-Reggiano, reserved liquid, and nutmeg to the meat mixture and knead the filling until smooth.

The filling will keep, refrigerated in an airtight container, for up to 10 days or frozen for up to 6 months. Transfer to a pastry bag, as needed.

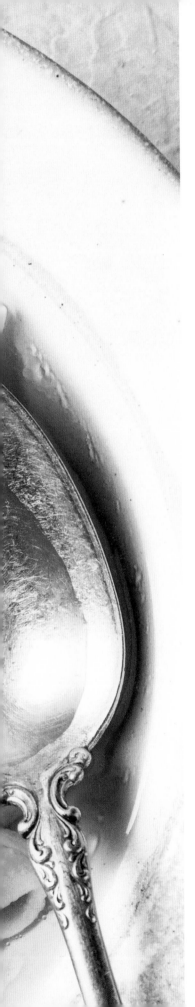

TORTELLINI IN BRODO

TORTELLINI IN MEAT BROTH

Tortellini *in brodo* IS Bologna. These savory little pasta parcels bobbing in a nutty, umami-rich broth can restore your whole soul. I'll never forget the first time I had the pasta. It was my first day at La Vecchia Scuola and the *maestra* announced we were having tortellini for lunch. I wondered out loud whether they might come drenched in ragù or swimming in a *crema di* Parmigiano-Reggiano sauce. I was summarily reprimanded for my ignorance. In Bologna, I was told, "tortellini" is code for tortellini *in brodo*. Always. There are no other acceptable ways to serve it. Never forget it.

SERVES 6

2¼ QT [2.1 L] BRODO DI CARNE (PAGE 237), OR LOW-SODIUM CHICKEN BROTH

KOSHER SALT

1 RECIPE TORTELLINI (PAGE 176)

1 CUP [100 G] FINELY GRATED PARMIGIANO-REGGIANO (OPTIONAL)

In a medium sauté pan or skillet over high heat, bring the *brodo* to a rolling boil. Delicately season the *brodo* with salt, keeping in mind the tortellini filling is salty. Add the tortellini and cook until tender, 2 to 3 minutes. Serve immediately with the Parmigiano-Reggiano on the side (if using).

TORTELLINI PASTICCIATA AL RAGÙ

TORTELLINI WITH MEAT SAUCE

Maestra Alessandra says only "mountain people" make this dish, a declaration that is not meant as a compliment. Like the Smeraldine (page 184), which diverge from the classic tortellini *in brodo*—the only acceptable method of serving tortellini according to bolognesi—*pasticciata* diverges from tradition, dressing the pasta with a rib-sticking dish, meat on meat on meat ragù. While tortellini *in brodo* is the crowning jewel of Bologna and puts the pasta on a pedestal, this recipe gives you the best of both worlds: stuffed pasta and savory sauce, a hearty combination that is satisfying on a cold night, whether you live in Italy or America, or anywhere in between.

SERVES 6

3½ CUPS [700 G] RAGÙ DELLA VECCHIA
SCUOLA (PAGE 90)

1 CUP [240 ML] HEAVY CREAM

KOSHER SALT

1 RECIPE TORTELLINI (PAGE 176)

1 CUP [100 G] FINELY GRATED
PARMIGIANO-REGGIANO

In a large sauté pan or skillet over medium heat, bring the ragù to a simmer and cook for about 3 minutes. Add the cream, return the mixture to a simmer, and season with salt. Set the sauce aside.

Bring a large pot of water to a rolling boil over high heat. Season the water with salt (see page 25). When the salt dissolves, add the tortellini and cook until tender, 2 to 3 minutes.

Meanwhile, return the sauce to medium heat. Using a spider, transfer the pasta to the sauce and swirl gently to coat. Add some pasta cooking water, as needed, to loosen the sauce. Serve immediately with the Parmigiano-Reggiano sprinkled on top.

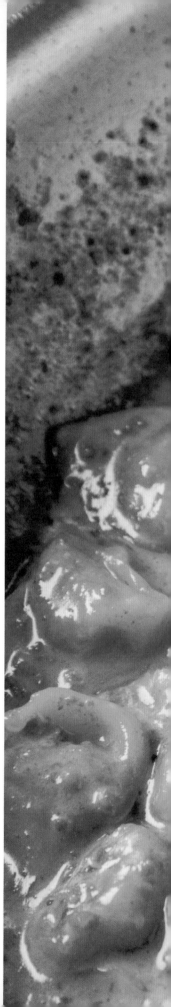

SMERALDINE ALLA PANNA

GREEN TORTELLINI WITH CREAM SAUCE

When Maestra Alessandra was young, she worked for a time as a *sfoglina* in Rome. She was horrified to find there the tortellini served swimming in cream sauce. As a Bologna native, any pairing but tortellini in *brodo* was considered blasphemous. Eventually, she invented *smeraldine* ("little emeralds")—basically, tortellini made with Spinach Dough—her version of a compromise with tradition. The green dough contrasted with the white cream sauce and she changed the filling to work better with the spinach and cream flavors.

SERVES 6

1 QT [960 ML] HEAVY CREAM

2 CUPS [480 ML] BRODO DI CARNE (PAGE 237), OR LOW-SODIUM CHICKEN BROTH

KOSHER SALT

1 RECIPE TORTELLINI (PAGE 176) MADE WITH SFOGLIA VERDE AGLI SPINACI (PAGE 42) AND FILLED WITH RIPIENO PER SMERALDINE (PAGE 179)

¾ CUP [75 G] FINELY GRATED PARMIGIANO-REGGIANO

In a large sauté pan or skillet over medium heat, simmer the cream until it is reduced by half, about 5 minutes. Add 1½ cups [360 ml] of *brodo*, return the mixture to a simmer, and season with salt. Set the sauce aside.

Bring a large pot of water to a rolling boil over high heat. Season the water with salt (see page 25). When the salt dissolves, add the tortellini and cook until tender, 2 to 3 minutes.

Return the sauce to medium heat. Using a spider, transfer the pasta to the sauce, being careful not to carry over any pasta cooking water. Bring to a simmer and cook for 2 minutes, swirling occasionally. Add ¼ cup [25 g] of Parmigiano-Reggiano and continue swirling to incorporate. Add the remaining ½ cup [120 ml] *brodo*, as needed, to loosen the sauce. Serve immediately with the remaining Parmigiano-Reggiano sprinkled on top.

Laboratori

In Bologna, pasta isn't just a meal—it's the city's lifeblood. Walk the streets of the historic center and you won't go more than a few hundred yards without seeing it displayed in a storefront, advertised on a billboard, or even immortalized in graffiti. You can see the craft behind it in action at the city's many *laboratori*, where pasta is mixed, rolled, cut, and shaped by hand. Some *laboratori* sell to the public onsite or at their own shops or eateries nearby and will even let you watch the pasta being made; others exclusively supply trattorias and/or prefer to work behind closed doors. These are a few I love.

BRUNO E FRANCO, VIA SAN SIMONE 2/A

The Bruno e Franco *laboratorio*, which doubles as a school, is on the third floor (second in Italian terms), so you have to buzz to get in. The *sfogline*—Grazia, Angela, Monica, and Mara—expertly roll and shape pasta on cherry wood using *mattarelli* carved around the turn of the twentieth century. You can take a class there or just stop by to watch them work, but to buy their wonderful pastas (tortellini, *cannelloni*, gnocchi, and other varieties), you must go to nearby Bruno e Franco on Via Guglielmo Oberdan 16, which is basically a *salumeria*.

TRATTORIA ANNA MARIA, VIA DELLE BELLE ARTI 17/A

Trattoria Anna Maria serves dozens of pasta dishes a day. Each tortellino or tagliatella strand is handcrafted a one-minute walk away in a yellow-hued workshop whose color scheme mirrors the tint of the wide pasta sheets rolled out by the *sfogline*. The *laboratorio* is closed to the public, but, luckily, anyone can dine at the trattoria.

LA VECCHIA SCUOLA BOLOGNESE, VIA STALINGRADO 81

Strange as it may sound, Maestra Alessandra's *laboratorio* is now in a circus tent well outside the city. She moved there from her original location near downtown Bologna, where I spent so much time, after a property dispute. Aside from that, not much has changed. The *maestra* and her family continue to run their pasta shop/school/informal restaurant and at 1 p.m.-ish every day, a few people come for lunch to eat the students' "mistakes." (There's no better way to learn how *not* to make pasta than to see your hard work thrown into the scrap bin and sold for cheap to diners.) Whether you visit for lunch or a lesson—she teaches amateurs and professional chefs alike—be sure to ask if you can buy some pasta *a portare via* (to take away).

SORPRE

Think of *sorpresine*, or little surprises, as a variation of tortellini, but without filling. The first time I encountered them was the day the mortadella delivery didn't show up at La Scuola. I figured the *maestra* would be livid, but she took it in stride and rather than fill pasta parcels as we would have for tortellini *in brodo*, we folded pasta squares into a sort of ridged ring and cooked them in a light vegetable broth. *Sorpresine* are an economic compromise for those who don't have—or cannot afford—filling, that don't sacrifice flavor, which comes from the broths they are paired with.

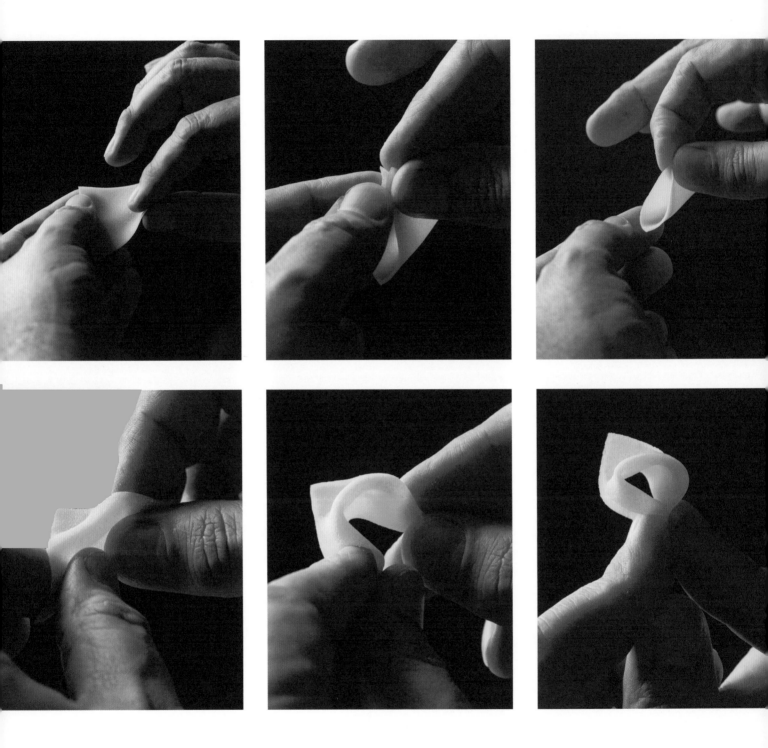

SORPRESINE

MAKES ABOUT 710 G [25 OZ], SERVING 6

1 RECIPE SFOGLIA ALL'UOVO (PAGE 38),
AT ROOM TEMPERATURE

"00" FLOUR, FOR DUSTING

Roll one dough ball to a thickness of
4 Post-it® Notes on a lightly floured
work surface (see page 50) and begin
cutting immediately. Set an accordion
pastry cutter to 1¼ in [3 cm]. Use firm,
even pressure to cut the *sfoglia* into
strips, moving south to north. The
edge of the pastry cutter should graze
the west edge of the *sfoglia*. Beginning at the bottom edge of the *sfoglia*,
use firm, even pressure to cut it into
strips, east to west. Clear away any
irregular pieces and add them to your
maltagliati pile (see page 100).

Cover the *sfoglia* with a clean plastic
trash can liner, leaving only a single
row exposed.

SHAPE THE SORPRESINE: Orient the
pasta as a diamond on the palm of
one hand. Using the thumb and index
finger of the opposite hand, fold the
southern tip of the diamond and join
it to the northern tip, forming an
open, empty purse. Using the same
two fingers, seal the pasta, just at the
top, pressing it to a single thickness
(see page 24).

Transfer the pasta to the other hand
and insert an index finger into either
end of the pasta tube. Pull the pointed
pasta flaps away from the sealed end
and join them, pressing the pasta to a
single thickness.

As each *sorpresina* is shaped, place it
on a clean work surface, taking care
not to let it touch the other pieces.
Repeat the shaping for the remaining *sfoglia*, working one row at a
time. Allow the shaped pasta to dry,
uncovered, on your work surface
for about 15 minutes. The *sorpresine*
are now ready to use, or you can dry
completely and store in an airtight
container for up to 2 weeks.

Repeat the process with the remaining dough ball.

SORPRESINE IN BRODO

SORPRESINE IN MEAT BROTH

This dish is basically a faster and easier version of Tortellini in Brodo (page 181). It is a great warm-up for pasta makers looking to improve their dexterity and can be whipped up in under 10 minutes, provided you have some broth and Egg Dough on hand. If you want to enrich the dish, crack an egg into the hot broth after adding the pasta and stir rapidly with a fork.

SERVES 6

2.5 QT [2.3 L] BRODO DI CARNE (PAGE 237), OR LOW-SODIUM CHICKEN BROTH

KOSHER SALT

1 RECIPE SORPRESINE (SEE PAGE 192)

½ CUP [50 G] FINELY GRATED PARMIGIANO-REGGIANO (OPTIONAL)

Place the *brodo* in a medium sauté pan or skillet and season with salt. Bring to a boil over high heat. Add the *sorpresine* and cook until tender, 2½ to 3 minutes. Serve immediately with the Parmigiano-Reggiano on the side (if using).

MINESTRA DI VERURDA CON SORPRESINE

SORPRESINE IN VEGETABLE BROTH

Bologna's cold winter months are dominated by hardy vegetables, such as bitter leafy greens and sweet heads of cabbage. What is nice about this soup is that it's warming and filling without being heavy.

SERVES 6

2 TBSP STRUTTO

ONE 3 IN [7.5 CM] PARMIGIANO-REGGIANO RIND

3 CELERY STALKS, DICED

1 LARGE CARROT, DICED

1 LARGE ONION, FINELY DICED

1 SMALL FENNEL BULB, OUTER LAYER DISCARDED, FINELY DICED

1 BUNCH SWISS CHARD, LEAVES STEMMED AND STEMS SLICED INTO ⅓ IN [0.8 CM] PIECES

LEAVES FROM 1 LARGE BUNCH FRESH FLAT-LEAF PARSLEY

1 FRESH BAY LEAF, TORN, OR 1 DRIED BAY LEAF, WHOLE

KOSHER SALT

SCANT TSP FRESHLY GROUND BLACK PEPPER

½ HEAD CABBAGE, CUT INTO SLIGHTLY LARGER THAN BITE–SIZE PIECES

3 QT [2.8 L] BRODO DI CARNE (PAGE 237), OR LOW-SODIUM CHICKEN BROTH

1 RECIPE SORPRESINE (SEE PAGE 192)

1 CUP [100 G] FINELY GRATED PARMIGIANO-REGGIANO

In a large pot over medium-high heat, melt the *strutto*. Add the Parmigiano-Reggiano rind, stirring continuously, until softened, about 2 minutes. Add the celery, carrot, onion, fennel, chard stems, and parsley. Cook until the onion is translucent, about 8 minutes. Add the bay leaf, season with salt and the pepper, and stir to combine. Add the cabbage and chard leaves. Cook until the chard is wilted, about 3 minutes.

Add the *brodo*, turn the heat to high, and bring the mixture to a boil. Reduce the heat to the lowest setting and simmer, uncovered, until the cabbage is tender, 45 minutes to 1 hour. Add the *sorpresine* and cook until tender, 2½ to 3 minutes. Serve immediately with the Parmigiano-Reggiano on the side.

CESTINI

Cestini, like *strichetti* (see page 108) and *caramelle* (see page 212), are a relatively modern shape. All over north-eastern Italy you find these filled pasta parcels served with sauces that mirror or complement their fillings. The shaping technique, which produces roughly pyramid-shaped pasta, is unique to the Spisni family; I adapt it here and pair it with the fillings and sauces I love.

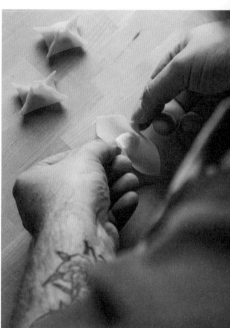

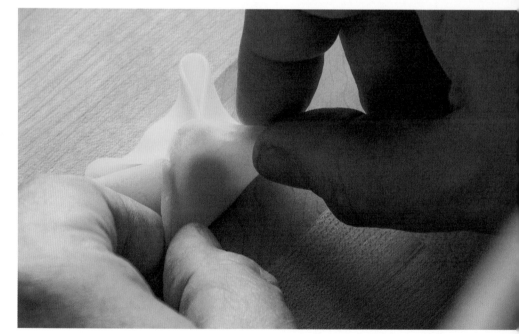

CESTINI

MAKES ABOUT 1.4 KG [49 OZ], INCLUDING FILLING, SERVING 6

1 RECIPE SFOGLIA ALL'UOVO (PAGE 38), AT ROOM TEMPERATURE

"00" FLOUR, FOR DUSTING

1 RECIPE RIPIENO OF CHOICE: RIPIENO DI ASPARAGI, RIPIENO DI SQUACQUERONE, OR RIPIENO DI ZUCCHINE (PAGE 205)

Roll one dough ball to a thickness of 7 Post-it® Notes on a lightly floured work surface (see page 50). Set an accordion pastry cutter to 2½ in [6 cm]. Use firm and even pressure to cut the *sfoglia* into strips, moving from east to west. The edge of the pastry cutter should graze the edge of the *sfoglia* closest to your body. Beginning at the eastern edge, cut the *sfoglia* into strips going north to south. Clear away any irregular pieces and add them to your *malta-gliati* pile (see page 100). Cover the pasta squares with plastic, exposing only a single row at a time.

FILL THE CESTINI: Transfer your *ripieno* of choice to a pastry bag (no tip needed). Pipe a marble-size amount (about 1 tsp) of *ripieno* in the middle of each pasta piece. Repeat with the remaining rows, one at a time.

SHAPE THE CESTINI: Transfer one filled piece of pasta to a clean part of your work surface and orient as a diamond. Using the thumb and index finger of one hand, lift the north and south corners of the diamond and gently press them together to join. Meanwhile, lift the eastern tip to join the north and south tips. Press together the edges of the pasta pieces to close the flap openings. Repeat on the west side of the pasta shape. The result should be a "pasta parcel" with four closed seams and a square base. Repeat with the remaining filled pieces.

Transfer the shaped pasta to a clean work surface and let dry, uncovered, for 15 minutes. The *cestini* are ready to use now, or you can blanch them for future use (see page 136).

Meanwhile, repeat the process with the remaining dough ball.

RIPIENO DI ASPARAGI

ASPARAGUS FILLING

This creamy and pleasantly vegetal filling is the perfect match for Cestini agli Asparagi (page 206).

MAKES ABOUT 1½ LB [681 G]

1 LB [454 G] (ABOUT 1 BUNCH) ASPARAGUS, TRIMMED AND BLANCHED

¾ CUP [180 G] RICOTTA

½ CUP [50 G] FINELY GRATED PARMIGIANO-REGGIANO

KOSHER SALT

In the bowl of a food processor, combine the blanched asparagus, ricotta, Parmigiano-Reggiano, and 1½ tsp salt. Blend on high speed until very smooth, about 1 minute. Adjust the seasoning, as needed. Transfer the filling to a piping bag (no tip needed) and refrigerate for at least 1 hour before using.

The filling will keep, refrigerated in the piping bag (cover the exposed end) or an airtight container, for up to 3 days.

RIPIENO DI SQUACQUERONE

SQUACQUERONE FILLING

Squacquerone is a fresh spreadable cheese from Romagna with an incomparable creaminess and tanginess. Because it is highly perishable, it is difficult to find outside of Italy. (I'd say it is worth a trip there just to eat it.) It might not be quite the same, but this recipe is still delicious if you substitute *crescenza* (also known as *stracchino*), *robiola*, or even a domestically produced triple-cream cheese.

MAKES ABOUT 1½ LB [681 G]

SCANT 1 LB [450 G] SQUACQUERONE

½ CUP [120 G] RICOTTA

1 CUP [100 G] FINELY GRATED PARMIGIANO-REGGIANO

In the bowl of a food processor, combine the *squacquerone*, ricotta, and Parmigiano-Reggiano. Blend on high speed until very smooth, about 1 minute. Transfer the filling to a piping bag (no tip needed) and refrigerate for at least 1 hour before using.

The filling will keep, refrigerated in the piping bag (cover the exposed end) or an airtight container, for up to 3 days.

RIPIENO DI ZUCCHINE

ZUCCHINI FILLING

This light *ripieno* is a summertime favorite when zucchini is so abundant. I sauté this seasonal ingredient for a fuller flavor.

MAKES ABOUT 1½ LB [681 G]

2 TBSP UNSALTED BUTTER

1 LB [454 G] ZUCCHINI, TRIMMED, CUT INTO ¾ IN [2 CM] SLICES

KOSHER SALT

10 FRESH BASIL LEAVES

½ CUP [120 G] RICOTTA

⅔ CUP [66 G] FINELY GRATED PARMIGIANO-REGGIANO

In a large sauté pan or skillet over medium heat, melt the butter until frothy and golden. Add the zucchini, season with salt, and cook, stirring until golden, 6 to 8 minutes. Set aside to cool on a parchment paper–lined sheet pan.

In the bowl of a food processor, combine the zucchini, basil, ricotta, Parmigiano-Reggiano, and 1½ tsp salt. Blend on high speed until very smooth, about 1 minute. Adjust the seasoning as needed. Transfer the filling to a piping bag (no tip needed) and refrigerate for at least 1 hour before using.

The filling will keep, refrigerated in the piping bag (cover the exposed end) or an airtight container, for up to 3 days.

CESTINI AGLI ASPARAGI

ASPARAGUS CESTINI

This filled pasta unites one of my favorite spring vegetables with Parmigiano-Reggiano. Each spring, they appear together across the Italian peninsula in a variety of ways, including in pastas and risottos. The asparagus and salty cheese contrast beautifully. Be sure to time boiling the pasta with making the sauce so you can emulsify it with some of the starchy pasta cooking water prior to adding the pasta.

SERVES 6

3 TBSP [42 G] UNSALTED BUTTER

1 LB [454 G] (ABOUT 1 BUNCH) ASPARAGUS, CUT ON A BIAS INTO 1 IN [2.5 CM] PIECES

KOSHER SALT

1 RECIPE CESTINI (PAGE 202) FILLED WITH RIPIENO DI ASPARAGI (PAGE 205)

½ CUP [50 G] FINELY GRATED PARMIGIANO-REGGIANO

In a large sauté pan or skillet over medium-high heat, melt the butter until frothy and golden. Add the asparagus and cook until just caramelized, about 1 minute. Set aside.

Bring a large pot of water to a rolling boil over high heat. Season the water with salt (see page 25). When the salt dissolves, add the *cestini* and cook for 2 to 2½ minutes until tender.

Meanwhile, return the pan with the asparagus to medium heat. Add ¼ cup [60 ml] of pasta cooking water and swirl to emulsify. Using a spider, transfer the pasta to the sauce, swirling the pasta in the pan to coat. Serve immediately with the Parmigiano-Reggiano sprinkled on top.

Cestini are delicate, so you don't want to disturb them too much by stirring with a utensil when you combine them with the sauce. Instead, swirl the pan to move the sauce over the *cestini*. This will coat them.

CESTINI ALLO SQUACQUERONE E BATTUTO DI RUCOLA

CESTINI WITH SQUACQUERONE AND ARUGULA PESTO

In Bologna pesto is called *battuto*, which is not the only thing that sets it apart from its basil-based counterpart from Genova. Bolognese *battuto* can feature any herb that grows in abundance in and around Bologna. In this recipe, it's arugula, and the piquant filling (see page 205) complements the spicy, herbaceous flavor of the arugula.

SERVES 6

KOSHER SALT

1 LB [454 G] ARUGULA

1 GARLIC CLOVE

1¼ CUPS [125 G] FINELY GRATED PARMIGIANO-REGGIANO

2 CUPS [480 ML] EXTRA-VIRGIN OLIVE OIL

1 RECIPE CESTINI (PAGE 202) FILLED WITH RIPIENO DI SQUACQUERONE (PAGE 205)

In a large bowl, prepare an ice bath and set aside.

Bring a large pot of water to a rolling boil over high heat. Season the water with salt (see page 25). When the salt dissolves, add the arugula and blanch until bright green, about 30 seconds. In a fine-mesh strainer, drain the arugula, then set the strainer in the ice bath to stop the cooking process.

Once the arugula is completely cooled, squeeze out all the water and transfer it to the bowl of a food processor. Add the garlic, ¾ cup [75 g] of Parmigiano-Reggiano, and the oil. Pulse until roughly chopped and season with salt. Transfer the pesto to a large bowl and set aside.

Bring another large pot of water to a rolling boil over high heat. Season the water with salt (see page 25). When the salt dissolves, add the *cestini* and cook, stirring occasionally, until tender, 2 to 2½ minutes. Using a spider, transfer the pasta to the pesto, tossing gently to coat. Serve immediately with the remaining ½ cup [50 g] of Parmigiano-Reggiano sprinkled on top.

The pesto will keep, refrigerated in an airtight container, for up to 3 days.

CESTINI DI ZUCCHINE, GUANCIALE, E FIORI DI ZUCCA

CESTINI WITH GUANCIALE AND ZUCCHINI FLOWERS

Zucchini are so abundant in summer that I have to get creative with how to use them all. Their flowers are harder to come by. If you're lucky enough to have a garden, growing your own zucchini is the best way to get them. Otherwise, make friends with your local farmer or farm stand and request that they set some flowers aside for you if they don't normally sell them. Be sure to time boiling the pasta with making the sauce so you can emulsify it with some of the starchy pasta cooking water prior to adding the pasta.

SERVES 6

6 OZ [170 G] GUANCIALE, CUT INTO ¼ IN [6 MM] BATONS

24 ZUCCHINI FLOWERS, CLEANED (SEE SIDEBAR)

KOSHER SALT

1 RECIPE CESTINI (PAGE 202) FILLED WITH RIPIENO DI ZUCCHINE (PAGE 205)

½ CUP PLUS 2 TBSP [62.5 G] FINELY GRATED PARMIGIANO-REGGIANO

In a large sauté pan or skillet over medium heat, cook the guanciale until lightly golden and crispy and the fat has rendered, about 2 minutes. Add the zucchini flowers and stir them in the rendered fat until they wilt, about 15 seconds. Set the sauce aside.

Bring a large pot of water to a rolling boil over high heat. Season the water with salt (see page 25). When the salt dissolves, add the *cestini* and cook until tender, 2 to 2½ minutes.

Meanwhile, return the sauce to medium heat. Add ¼ cup [60 ml] of pasta cooking water and swirl to emulsify. Add 2 Tbsp of Parmigiano-Reggiano, swirling to combine. Using a spider, transfer the pasta to the sauce, swirling the pasta in the pan to coat. Serve immediately with the remaining ½ cup [50 g] Parmigiano-Reggiano sprinkled on top.

How to Clean and Store Zucchini Flowers

Carefully remove and discard the pollen sacs from the flowers. Detach the entire flower from its stem, if there is one, and tear the flower in half, lengthwise. (Male flowers grow on the plant and have stems; female flowers are attached to the zucchini itself, so they don't have stems.) Zucchini flowers don't last long once they've been harvested, so it's best to use them within a day or two of harvesting or buying them. Keep the flowers loosely wrapped with paper towels and in a cool, dry place away from the sun until needed.

CARAME

Who doesn't have nostalgic feelings for wrapped candy? You pull the ends of these cute little parcels to reveal a sweet surprise. Keep that shape in mind—though don't do any such pulling!—when making *caramelle*, a pasta shape that evokes old-school candy.

Although they are late-twentieth century inventions, *caramelle* shouldn't be dismissed as frivolous. They are fun to make and, once you master the technique, offer a highly satisfying achievement to add to your homemade pasta arsenal.

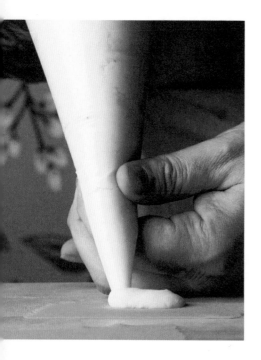

CARAMELLE

MAKES ABOUT 1.4 KG [49 OZ],
INCLUDING FILLING, SERVING 6

1 RECIPE SFOGLIA ALL'UOVO (PAGE 38),
AT ROOM TEMPERATURE

"00" FLOUR, FOR DUSTING

1 RECIPE RIPIENO OF CHOICE: RIPIENO AI
QUATTRO FORMAGGI, RIPIENO AI CARCIOFI,
OR RIPIENO DI PATATE (PAGE 218–19)

Roll one dough ball to a thickness of 7 Post-it® Notes on a lightly floured work surface (see page 50). Set an accordion pastry cutter to 2 in [5 cm]. Use firm and even pressure to cut the *sfoglia* horizontally into 2 in [5 cm] thick strips, cutting from east to west. With a fluted pastry cutter, use firm and even pressure to cut the *sfoglia* into 4 in [10 cm] pieces, cutting from south to north.

Clear away any irregular pieces and add them to your *maltagliati* pile (see page 100).

FILL THE CARAMELLE: Transfer your *ripieno* of choice to a pastry bag (no tip needed). Lay a clean, unscented plastic trash can liner over the pasta squares, exposing only a single row at a time. Pipe a 1½ by ¼ in [4 cm by 6 mm] thick strip of *ripieno* into the middle 1 in [2.5 cm] of each dough square; leave the opposing ends of the horizontally oriented pasta rectangle unfilled. Repeat with the remaining rows, one row at a time.

SHAPE THE CARAMELLE: Roll the bottom edge of the pasta up and over the filling, tucking it under the filling. Roll it like a cigar on your work surface, ensuring the outer edge seam is centered directly beneath the pasta shape. Using your index fingers, press firmly where the dough meets the edge of the filling on both short ends. Using both hands, keep your index finger on the pinched impression around the filling. Place your thumb and middle finger in line with the index finger. Lift the edges of the dough, gathering and joining the folds. Pinch the joint, ensuring a single thickness (see page 24). Repeat with the remaining dough pieces.

Transfer the shaped pasta to a clean work surface and let dry, uncovered, for 15 minutes. The *caramelle* are ready to use now, or you can blanch them for future use (see page 136).

Meanwhile, repeat the process with the remaining dough ball.

RIPIENO AI QUATTRO FORMAGGI

FOUR CHEESE FILLING

I like the combination of cheeses here, but you can certainly experiment. Adding a bit of truffle takes the filling to another level, but it's wonderful without it, too.

MAKES ABOUT 1½ LB [681 G]

4 OZ [113.5 G] TOMINO OR BRIE

9 OZ [255 G] ROBIOLA

9 OZ [255 G] CRESCENZA (STRACCHINO), OR CREAM CHEESE

⅔ CUP [66 G] FINELY GRATED PARMIGIANO-REGGIANO

SHAVINGS FROM THE OUTSIDE OF ONE 1¾ OZ [50 G] BLACK TRUFFLE (OPTIONAL; SEE CARAMELLE CON QUATTRO FORMAGGI E TARTUFO HEADNOTE, PAGE 222)

In the bowl of a food processor, combine the *tomino*, *robiola*, *crescenza*, and Parmigiano-Reggiano and process until smooth, about 2 minutes. Add the truffle shavings (if using) and pulse to combine. Transfer the filling to a piping bag (no tip needed).

The filling will keep, refrigerated in the piping bag (cover the exposed end) or an airtight container, for up to 3 days.

RIPIENO AI CARCIOFI

ARTICHOKE FILLING

If you're using this filling to make Caramelle ai Carciofi (page 220), cook the four artichokes called for in that recipe with the ones here.

MAKES ABOUT 1½ LB [681 G]

2 TBSP UNSALTED BUTTER

1 GARLIC CLOVE, SMASHED

½ YELLOW ONION, SLICED

1 SPRIG THYME

½ CUP [120 ML] DRY WHITE WINE

3 QT [2.8 L] COLD WATER

KOSHER SALT

1½ LB [681 G] BABY ARTICHOKES, CLEANED (SEE PAGE 220)

3½ OZ [100 G] RICOTTA

⅔ CUP [66 G] FINELY GRATED PARMIGIANO-REGGIANO

In a large heavy-bottomed pot over medium-high heat, melt the butter until frothy and golden. Add the garlic, onion, and thyme and cook until the onion is translucent, about 8 minutes. Add the wine and cook until the alcohol aroma dissipates and the liquid has reduced by half, about 2 minutes. Add the cold water, bring to a rolling boil over high heat, and season with salt (see page 25). Add the artichokes and return the water to a boil. Turn the heat to medium and cook until the artichokes are fork-tender, 12 to 15 minutes.

RIPIENO DI PATATE

POTATO FILLING

Drain the artichokes, discarding the liquid. Remove and discard the thyme sprig and transfer the artichokes to the bowl of a food processor. Process until smooth, about 1 minute, then transfer the artichoke mixture to a large bowl. Fold in the ricotta and Parmigiano-Reggiano, cover, and set aside until cool. Transfer the filling to a piping bag (no tip needed) and refrigerate for at least 2 hours before using.

The filling will keep, refrigerated in the piping bag (cover the exposed end) or an airtight container, for up to 3 days.

I like to kick up the creamy and buttery filling with a pinch of nutmeg.

MAKES ABOUT 1½ LB [681 G]

1 LB [605 G] YUKON GOLD POTATOES, PEELED AND QUARTERED

1 TBSP KOSHER SALT, PLUS MORE FOR SEASONING

½ CUP [125 G] RICOTTA

⅔ CUP [66 G] FINELY GRATED PARMIGIANO-REGGIANO

1 LARGE EGG

3 SMALL PINCHES OF NUTMEG, PREFERABLY FRESHLY GRATED

In a large pot, combine the potatoes with enough cold water to cover and bring to a rolling boil over high heat. Season the water with salt (see page 25), decrease the heat to medium, and simmer until fork-tender, about 20 minutes. Drain and set aside to cool completely, about 20 minutes.

Rice the potatoes or use a bench scraper to press them through a fine-mesh strainer into a large bowl. Add the 1 Tbsp salt, the ricotta, Parmigiano-Reggiano, egg, and nutmeg and stir to combine. Transfer the filling to a piping bag (no tip needed).

The filling will keep, refrigerated in the piping bag (cover the exposed end) or an airtight container, for up to 3 days. Bring to room temperature before using.

CARAMELLE AI CARCIOFI

CARAMELLE WITH ARTICHOKE FILLING

This recipe calls for a cooked artichoke filling, as well as a cooked artichoke sauce. If possible, kill two birds with one stone and cook the artichokes in this recipe with those you prepare for the Ripieno ai Carciofi (page 218).

SERVES 6

2 TBSP UNSALTED BUTTER

1 GARLIC CLOVE, SMASHED

½ YELLOW ONION, SLICED

1 SPRIG THYME

¾ CUP [180 ML] DRY WHITE WINE

3 QT [2.8 L] COLD WATER

KOSHER SALT

4 BABY ARTICHOKES, CLEANED (SEE SIDEBAR) AND CUT INTO ⅛ IN [3 MM] SLICES

5 OZ [140 G] PANCETTA, CUT INTO ¼ IN [6 MM] BATONS

1½ CUPS [360 ML] VEGETABLE BROTH

30 FRESH MINT LEAVES, TORN

1 RECIPE CARAMELLE (PAGE 216) FILLED WITH RIPIENO AI CARCIOFI (PAGE 218)

½ CUP [50 G] FINELY GRATED PARMIGIANO-REGGIANO

In a large heavy-bottomed sauté pan or skillet over medium-high heat, melt the butter until frothy and golden. Add the garlic, onion, and thyme and cook until the onion is translucent, about 8 minutes. Add ½ cup [120 ml] of the wine and cook until the alcohol aroma dissipates and the liquid has reduced by half, about 2 minutes.

Add the cold water and bring to a rolling boil over high heat. Season with salt (see page 25). When the salt dissolves, add the artichokes and return the water to a boil. Turn the heat to medium and cook until the artichokes are fork-tender, 12 to 15 minutes. Drain, discarding the liquid. Remove and discard the thyme sprig, then set the artichokes aside in a small bowl.

In a large sauté pan or skillet over medium heat, cook the pancetta until golden brown and crispy and the fat has rendered, about 4 minutes. Add the artichokes, season with salt, and cook, undisturbed, until golden brown, about 4 minutes. Add the remaining ¼ cup [60 ml] wine. Cook until the alcohol aroma evaporates and the liquid has reduced by half, about 2 minutes. Add the broth and cook until the liquid has reduced by half, 2 to 3 minutes, swirling to emulsify. Stir in the mint. Set the sauce aside.

Bring a large pot of water to a rolling boil over high heat. Season the water with salt (see page 25). When the salt dissolves, add the *caramelle* and cook until tender, about 2 minutes.

Meanwhile, return the sauce to medium heat. Using a spider, transfer the pasta to the sauce and gently stir to coat. Add some pasta cooking water, as needed, to loosen the sauce. Serve immediately with the Parmigiano-Reggiano sprinkled on top.

Cleaning Baby Artichokes

Fill a bowl of water and squeeze a halved lemon into the water, placing both halves in the water. Using gloved hands, tear off and discard the artichoke's outer leaves until you reach the tender inner leaves. Using a knife, peel off the stem's fibrous outer layer. Clip off and discard the top of the leaves. Baby artichokes are typically in season in May and June and again in September and October. If the artichokes are late in season, you'll need to remove choke, too. To do so, halve the artichoke lengthwise and use a melon baller to scoop out the fuzzy choke and any spiny bits. Set aside in the acidulated water.

They will keep, refrigerated in the lemon water, for up to 2 days.

CARAMELLE CON QUATTRO FORMAGGI E TARTUFO

CARAMELLE WITH FOUR CHEESES AND BLACK TRUFFLES

This is one of those dishes considered by many to be so decadent when served at a restaurant in the States, but it is actually pretty ordinary in north-central Italy in the fall, when black truffles are in season. That said, it is indulgent in that it calls for one whole truffle, although if you're going to splurge, I'd say you won't be disappointed here. Use a Microplane™ to grate off the exterior for the filling (see page 218), if you like, and slice the remainder with a mandoline or truffle slicer for the sauce and garnish. Not one bit will go to waste. Be sure to time boiling the pasta with making the sauce so you can emulsify it with some of the starchy pasta cooking water prior to adding the pasta.

SERVES 6

4 TBSP [56 G] UNSALTED BUTTER, CUT INTO PIECES

ONE 1¾ OZ [50 G] FRESH BLACK TRUFFLE, EXTERIOR SHAVED AND USED FOR RIPIENO AI QUATTRO FORMAGGI (PAGE 218), IF YOU LIKE

KOSHER SALT

1 RECIPE CARAMELLE (PAGE 216) FILLED WITH RIPIENO AI QUATTRO FORMAGGI (PAGE 218)

In a large sauté pan or skillet over low heat, melt the butter. Using a truffle shaver or mandoline, thinly shave half the truffle into the melted butter and heat for 30 seconds. Set the sauce aside.

Bring a large pot of water to a rolling boil over high heat. Season the water with salt (see page 25). When the salt dissolves, add the *caramelle* and cook until tender, about 2 minutes.

Meanwhile, return the sauce to medium heat. Add ¼ cup [60 ml] of pasta cooking water and swirl to emulsify, agitating it vigorously. Using a spider, transfer the pasta to the sauce and gently stir to coat. Serve immediately with the remaining truffle half shaved on top.

The Hunt for Truffles

Maurizio Lorenzini's leather European carry-all was grease stained. The famous truffle hunter was, otherwise, impeccably put together in freshly pressed head-to-toe camo, so the greasy satchel really caught my eye. When I met Maurizio in the hills outside Bologna 10 years ago, truffle season was in full swing and I was eager to see how he tracked down this wild fungus in the damp forests around the village of Savigno—and I wanted the story behind that bag.

For years I had been hearing about Maurizio and his knack for finding the region's best truffles, and I knew he had honed the craft alongside his father-in-law, foraging celebrity Adriano Bartolini. It didn't come as a surprise, then, that truffle hunting in Emilia-Romagna is a family business. So many Italian artisans I had met—from carpenters to cheesemongers—carried on a multi-generational tradition. Why would truffle hunting be any different? What I didn't know, until I met Maurizio and Adriano, was that the rule applied to animals, too.

On that damp day in October, Maurizio, Adriano, and I made the muddy trek into the forest with their dogs, Macchia and Pupa—daughter and mother. Just as Maurizio had learned from Adriano, so, too, had Macchia learned from Pupa. The four-member team was known across the region for their prowess in tracking down the finest truffles. The dogs, Lagotto Romagnolos, are naturally predisposed hunters. The breed has a keen sense of smell and an intense loyalty to their masters. It didn't hurt that Maurizio and Adriano knew just how to motivate their canines.

As we walked through the woods, Macchia and Pupa would stop in their tracks—nose to the ground—when they sensed a truffle. Then they would start digging, kicking up leaves and dirt as they excavated. Macchia, the younger of the two, was especially energetic. Maurizio would crouch down and put his face next to her paws and whisper, "*Dov'e', Macchia*?" (Where is it, Macchia?) When he thought she had dug far enough, he would pull her away by her collar and use a kind of flat, dull blade tethered to a stick to prod the earth. He would sniff a bit of the dirt and, if he thought there was a whole truffle down there, he would dig it up. If, instead, he sensed only a spore, he would re-cover it to let it grow. Either way, he'd pull a couple of mortadella cubes from his satchel and feed them to whichever dog led him to the spot. The dogs who worked for salami were the reason for the greasy bag.

CARAMELLE DI PATATE CON PORCINI

CARAMELLE WITH POTATO FILLING AND PORCINI MUSHROOMS

Potatoes and porcini are a classic autumn combination. If you can, purchase fresh porcini. If not, substitute the same amount of frozen porcini. (Before using, defrost them completely overnight in the refrigerator, uncovered, on an absorbant, non-terry cloth kitchen towel.

SERVES 6

4 TBSP [56 G] UNSALTED BUTTER

1 GARLIC CLOVE, SMASHED

ONE 1 IN [2.5 CM] PIECE OF ROSEMARY SPRIG

1 LB [454 G] FRESH PORCINI, CUT INTO ¼ IN [6 MM] SLICES

KOSHER SALT

¼ CUP [60 ML] DRY WHITE WINE

2 CUPS [480 ML] BRODO DI FUNGHI (PAGE 247)

1 RECIPE CARAMELLE (PAGE 216) FILLED WITH RIPIENO DI PATATE (PAGE 219)

½ CUP [50 G] FINELY GRATED PARMIGIANO-REGGIANO

In a large sauté pan or skillet over medium-high heat, melt 3 Tbsp of the butter until frothy and golden, 30 to 45 seconds. Add the garlic and rosemary and cook until fragrant, about 10 seconds. Add the porcini and toss in the melted butter to coat. Cook, without agitating, until the mushrooms are caramelized, about 2 minutes, and season with salt. Add the wine and cook until reduced by half, 2 to 3 minutes. Add the *brodo* and cook until reduced by half, 2 to 3 minutes more. Add the remaining 1 Tbsp butter and swirl to emulsify. Set the sauce aside.

Bring a large pot of water to a rolling boil over high heat. Season the water with salt (see page 25). When the salt dissolves, add the *caramelle* and cook until tender, about 2 minutes.

Meanwhile, return the sauce to medium heat. Using a spider, transfer the pasta to the sauce and gently stir to coat. Add some pasta cooking water, as needed, to loosen the sauce. Serve immediately with the Parmigiano-Reggiano sprinkled on top.

STROZZA

Strozzapreti (priest stranglers) are the first pasta shape you learn at La Vecchia Scuola (see page 186). It's made from a simple "00" Flour and Water Dough, so there's less risk of messing up than a richer, more expensive, egg-based *sfoglia*. In addition to being inexpensive to make, Flour and Water Dough is super easy to roll out, so use it to gain confidence in understanding a dough's consistency and to practice important pasta-making skills, such as the rolling technique, unfurling, and hand dexterity.

Strozzapreti, which take a number of forms throughout Italy—anything from short, twisted strands to bread dumplings—got their unique name from a myth. While traveling, a famished priest stopped at a convent where he demanded a plate of pasta from the sisters, which they dutifully provided. The gluttonous priest scarfed down the pasta at high speed and the *strozzapreti* lodged in his throat. The choking priest was saved by a swift smack to the back of the head—administered by a nun.

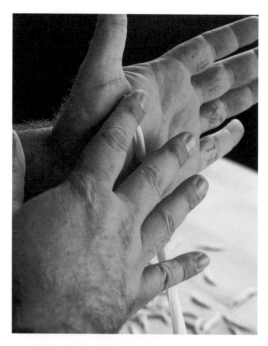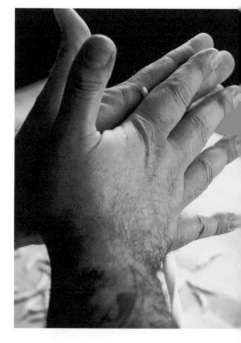

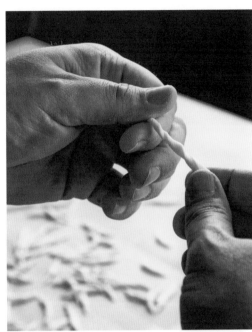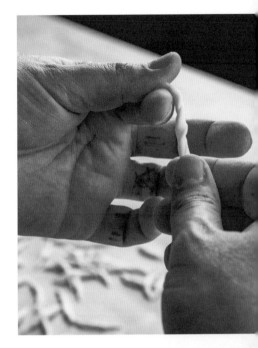
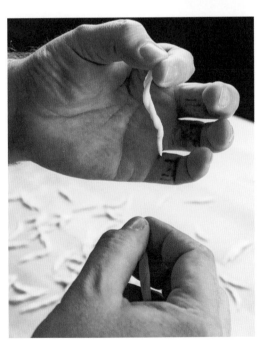

STROZZAPRETI

**MAKES ABOUT 680 G [24 OZ],
SERVING 6**

**1 RECIPE SFOGLIA DI ACQUA E FARINA
(PAGE 34)**

"00" FLOUR, FOR DUSTING

Roll one dough ball to a thickness of 6 Post-it® Notes on a lightly floured work surface (see page 50). Let it rest on the work surface, uncovered, for about 5 minutes.

Set an accordion pastry cutter to 1 in [2.5 cm]. Use firm and even pressure to cut the *sfoglia* into strips, moving from south to north until you cut about 16 to 18 strips. If you don't have an accordion pastry cutter, use a sharp knife to cut the *sfoglia* into 1 in [2.5 cm] wide strips.

Cover the strips with a clean, unscented plastic trash can liner, leaving the first strip exposed. Place the exposed pasta strip in one hand, laying it across your palm. Using the index finger of your opposite hand, roll the pasta to the opposite index finger. Wrap the pasta over that index finger as though you are tying a shoe-lace. Pinch and twist the rolled pasta while pulling gently to detach the pasta piece (1.5 to 2 in [3.8 to 5 cm] long), letting it drop onto your work surface. Repeat with the remaining *sfoglia* strips, folding back the plastic each time to expose the next strip.

Transfer the shaped pasta to a clean work surface and let dry, uncovered, for 10 to 15 minutes.

Meanwhile, repeat the rolling, shaping, and drying process with the remaining dough ball. The *strozza-preti* are now ready to use.

Strozzapreti don't keep well in the refrigerator. If you're not going to use them now, arrange them on a parchment paper–lined tray so they don't touch. Tightly cover the tray with plastic wrap and freeze the pasta until hard. Transfer the frozen pasta to a freezer bag or plastic container and keep frozen for up to 1 month. There's no need to thaw the pasta before cooking, but increase the cooking time by 1 minute.

STROZZAPRETI AL LESSO RIPASSATO

STROZZAPRETI WITH SIMMERED MEAT

The beauty of this dish is that it utilizes all the tender simmered meat that's left when you make Brodo di Carne (page 237), which clings perfectly to the pasta strands. Though a lot of the meat flavor is absorbed by the *brodo*, the addition of tomato here kicks up the meat flavor, seasoning it in a way. This resourcefulness and practicality isn't unique to Bologna. All over Italy, cooks pull meat from broth bones and add it to pasta sauces or fry it in *strutto* to serve over a hunk of bread or between two slices. The meat moistened with some of the *brodo* is also great spooned over soft polenta or slathered on toasted bread. Nothing goes to waste.

SERVES 6

2 OZ [56 G] STRUTTO

1 GARLIC CLOVE, SMASHED

½ CUP [20 G] CHOPPED FRESH FLAT-LEAF PARSLEY

2 CUPS [450 G] PASSATA DI POMODORO (PAGE 236)

BRAISED CHICKEN FROM BRODO DI CARNE (PAGE 237), MEAT PULLED FROM THE CARCASS AND SHREDDED

BRAISED BEEF SHANK FROM BRODO DI CARNE (PAGE 237), MEAT PULLED FROM THE BONE AND SHREDDED

2 CUPS [480 ML] BRODO DI CARNE (PAGE 237)

KOSHER SALT

FRESHLY GROUND BLACK PEPPER

1 RECIPE STROZZAPRETI (PAGE 232)

1 CUP [100 G] FINELY GRATED PARMIGIANO-REGGIANO

In a large heavy-bottomed pot over medium heat, melt the *strutto*. Add the garlic and parsley and cook just until the garlic begins to take color, about 1½ minutes. Add the *passata* and bring it to a rapid simmer. Stir in the chicken and beef. Add the *brodo* and return the mixture to a simmer. Season with salt and pepper. Set the sauce aside.

Bring a large pot of water to a rolling boil over high heat. Season the water with salt (see page 25). When the salt dissolves, add the *strozzapreti* and cook until tender, 1 to 1½ minutes.

Meanwhile, return the sauce to medium heat. Using a spider, transfer the pasta to the sauce and stir to coat. Add some pasta cooking water, as needed, to loosen the sauce. Serve immediately with the Parmigiano-Reggiano sprinkled on top.

The sauce will keep, refrigerated in an airtight container, for up to 7 days or frozen for up to 6 months.

PASSATA DI POMODORO

TOMATO SAUCE

Each August, bolognese families gather to harvest, blanch, peel, and bottle tomatoes to use throughout the year. If you have your own preserved tomatoes, this would be a great place to use them. Otherwise, opt for a high quality canned version. I like the San Marzano variety for my *passata* and Bianco DiNapoli is my favorite domestic producer (see Canned Tomatoes, page 30).

MAKES ABOUT 3 QT [2.8 L]

10 LB [ABOUT 4.5 KG] CANNED WHOLE TOMATOES

¼ CUP [60 ML] EXTRA-VIRGIN OLIVE OIL

1 GARLIC CLOVE, SMASHED

3 SPRIGS MARJORAM

1 TBSP KOSHER SALT

Pass the tomatoes through a food mill into a large bowl. Alternatively, in the bowl of a food processor, pulse the tomatoes on high speed until very smooth, about 1 minute.

In a large pot over medium-low heat, heat the oil until it begins to shimmer. Add the garlic and marjoram and cook until fragrant, about 1 minute. Add the tomatoes and salt and cook until the tomatoes have lost their raw flavor and the sauce has reduced slightly, about 30 minutes.

The sauce will keep, refrigerated in an airtight container, for up to 5 days or frozen for up to 6 months.

BRODO DI CARNE

MEAT BROTH

Brodo di Carne is the backbone of so many recipes in this book. You'll use it in the most traditional dish, Tortellini in Brodo (page 181), but also as a building block for many others. The simplicity of a great *brodo* speaks volumes. The one I make is the *maestra's*—it's how she makes it and how her family has for generations.

Everyone's *brodo* is their own, and small tweaks can make each unique. One family might use more carrots, another more onion. One might use beef neck, another shank. I go for a chicken and veal shank combo, because I want to evoke la *bell'aria*—"the smell of the air" in Bologna, the aromas that typified my favorite versions eaten there. A by-product of Brodo di Carne is a lot of simmered meat that is often used as the basis for Lesso Ripassato (page 235), a sauce for *strozzapreti*.

Great *brodo* is achieved with patience and time. It takes a full 24 hours to develop the beautiful, round, fortifying flavors. If you rush it, it will taste rushed. You must cook it overnight, so just make sure the area around the stove and the pot is clear and that the heat is very low.

The recipe yields much more *brodo* than you need for any single recipe in the book. This is one of those batch recipes (see page 25) that bolognesi make in abundance, and so do I, especially because it is the amount of *brodo* that results from simmering one whole chicken. Use any leftovers by making other recipes that call for Brodo di Carne, adding to soups, or freezing what you don't need for future use.

MAKES ABOUT 9 QT [8.6 L]

ONE 3½ LB [1.6 KG] WHOLE CHICKEN (PREFERABLY ORGANIC), RINSED AND PATTED DRY

ONE 1 LB [454 G] VEAL OR BEEF SHANK

2 CELERY STALKS

1 LARGE CARROT

1 LARGE YELLOW ONION, HALVED

6 QT [5.7 L] COLD WATER

In a large heavy-bottomed pot over low heat, combine the chicken, veal shank, celery, carrot, and onion. Add the water and bring to a simmer. Decrease the heat as needed to maintain a bare simmer and cook, uncovered, for about 24 hours. The *brodo* can bubble occasionally, but do not boil, stir, or disturb it in any way.

After 24 hours, the *brodo* will be golden and translucent and taste savory. Using a ladle, skim off the scum from the top of the *brodo* and discard. One ladleful at a time, pass the *brodo* through a fine-mesh strainer or chinois into a large container or several smaller ones. *Do not pour it*— the force will push impurities through the strainer and con-taminate the *brodo*. Reserve the meats (discarding the bones) and vegetables for Lesso Ripassato (page 235; they will keep, refrigerated in an airtight container, for up to 3 days). If you are not using the *brodo* now, cool it completely over an ice bath before storing.

The *brodo* will keep, refriger-ated in an airtight container, for up to 10 days or frozen for up to 3 months.

STROZZAPRETI AL FRIGGIONE

STROZZAPRETI WITH TOMATO ONION SAUCE

Never ever tell a person from Bologna that you have used *friggione*, a rich, flavorful stew, as a pasta sauce. There, *friggione* is only employed as a *contorno* (side dish), to accompany a main dish. It is served unceremoniously on a plate all by itself. The lack of adornment doesn't mean an absence of reverence. On the contrary, *friggione* is seen as whole on its own. Combining it with pasta is nothing short of blasphemous, so, even though the result is unbelievably delicious, let's keep this recipe between us.

SERVES 6

6 TO 8 LARGE (6 LB [2.7 KG]) YELLOW ONIONS, THINLY SLICED

1 TBSP KOSHER SALT, PLUS MORE FOR SEASONING

1 TBSP SUGAR

3 TBSP STRUTTO, OR UNSALTED BUTTER

2 CUPS [450 G] PASSATA DI POMODORO (PAGE 236)

1 RECIPE STROZZAPRETI (PAGE 232)

1 CUP [100 G] FINELY GRATED PARMIGIANO-REGGIANO

In a large bowl, combine the onions, 1 Tbsp salt, and the sugar. Using your hands, toss to combine. Cover the bowl with plastic wrap and set aside for 4 hours to break down the onions and extract their moisture.

In a large heavy-bottomed pot over medium heat, melt the *strutto*. Add the onion mixture and its liquid. Decrease the heat to low and cover the pot. Cook until the onions have released their liquid, about 1 hour. Using a wooden spoon, stir the onions occasionally, scraping the bottom of the pan to prevent them from sticking. Add a splash of water, as needed, if the onions stick.

Uncover the pot and cook, stirring frequently, until the onions and their liquid have reduced to the thickness of jam, about 1 hour more. The onions should be a deep blond color, but not yet browned. Stir in the *passata*. Cook until the sauce is thick and juicy, but not pasty, 45 minutes to 1 hour. Set the sauce aside.

Bring a large pot of water to a rolling boil over high heat. Season the water with salt (see page 25). When the salt dissolves, add the *strozzapreti* and cook until tender, 1 to 1½ minutes.

Meanwhile, return the sauce to medium heat. Using a spider, transfer the pasta to the sauce and stir to coat. Add some pasta cooking water, as needed, to loosen the sauce. Serve immediately with the Parmigiano-Reggiano sprinkled on top.

The sauce will keep, refrigerated in an airtight container, for up to 5 days.

STROZZAPRETI AL RAGÙ DI CONIGLIO

STROZZAPRETI WITH RABBIT RAGÙ

In Emilia-Romanga, this ragù is typically made with wild hare, but as that isn't always readily available elsewhere, I've substituted rabbit here. The fattier, less gamey meat yields a lighter, more supple sauce, making it ideal for lunch or a light dinner. You can use the sauce right away, but I think it's improved after sitting in the refrigerator overnight, or for up to 3 days. Just be sure to let it cool completely before refrigerating and keep it tightly covered.

MAKES 3½ QT SAUCE, SERVING 6

1 2.5 TO 3 LB [1.1 TO 1.4 KG] WHOLE RABBIT, WASHED AND PATTED DRY

KOSHER SALT

FRESHLY GROUND BLACK PEPPER

6 TBSP [84 G] UNSALTED BUTTER

3½ OZ [100 G] PANCETTA, DICED

6 TO 8 FRESH SAGE LEAVES, TORN

3 GARLIC CLOVES, MINCED

1 DRIED BAY LEAF

1 PINCH OF FENNEL POLLEN (OPTIONAL)

3 CELERY STALKS, FINELY DICED

1 MEDIUM YELLOW ONION, FINELY DICED

1 MEDIUM CARROT, FINELY DICED

1 SMALL FENNEL BULB, OUTER LAYER DISCARDED, FINELY DICED

2 CUPS [480 ML] DRY WHITE WINE

1.5 QT [1420 ML] BRODO DI CARNE (PAGE 237), OR BEEF CONSOMMÉ

1 RECIPE STROZZAPRETI (PAGE 232)

½ CUP [50 G] FINELY GRATED PARMIGIANO-REGGIANO

Season the rabbit all over with salt and pepper and set aside. In a large heavy-bottomed pot over medium-high heat, melt 4 Tbsp [56 g] of butter. Add the rabbit legs and sear on all sides until golden brown, about 6 minutes total. Transfer to a sheet tray and set aside.

Decrease the heat to low and add the pancetta. Cook, stirring frequently, until golden brown and crispy and the fat has rendered, about 4 minutes. Add the sage, garlic, bay leaf, and fennel pollen (if using) and cook until fragrant, about 1 minute. Increase the heat to medium and add the celery, onion, carrot, and fennel. Season with salt and cook until the vegetables are golden and tender, 15 to 20 minutes.

Add the wine and bring to a boil. Cook until the alcohol aroma dissipates and the liquid has reduced by half, about 2 minutes. Stir in the *brodo*. Return the mixture to a boil and transfer the rabbit back to the pot. Decrease the heat to low and half-cover the pot. Simmer until the legs are very tender and the meat is falling off the bone, 2 to 3 hours.

Remove the pot from the heat and gently transfer the rabbit to a platter to cool for about 15 minutes. When the rabbit is cool enough to handle, pull all the meat from the bones and roughly chop it, discarding the bones, paying special attention to the tiny

rib bones. Return the pot to medium heat. Bring the sauce to a rapid simmer and cook until the liquid is reduced by about half, 20 to 30 minutes more. Stir the chopped meat into the sauce and season with salt.

Transfer 5 cups [1.1 kg] of the sauce to a large sauté pan or skillet. (Store the extra sauce according to the instructions following.) Place the pan over medium heat. Bring the sauce to a rapid simmer and cook until the sauce reduces slightly, about 5 minutes. Add the remaining 2 Tbsp butter and swirl to emulsify. Set the sauce aside.

Bring a large pot of water to a rolling boil over high heat. Season the water with salt (see page 25). When the salt dissolves, add the *strozzapreti*. Cook until tender, 1 to 1½ minutes.

Meanwhile, return the sauce to medium heat. Using a spider, transfer the pasta to the sauce and stir to coat. Add some pasta cooking water, as needed, to loosen the sauce. Serve immediately with the Parmigiano-Reggiano sprinkled on top.

The sauce will keep, refrigerated in an airtight container, for up to 5 days or frozen for up to 6 months.

GNOCCHI DI

There isn't a single Italian region that doesn't have a dumpling of some kind and, thanks to its robust cow's milk cheese industry, Emilia-Romagna's native version includes ricotta, the byproduct of Parmigiano-Reggiano production. The aerated ricotta makes the dough light and supple. I like to use cow's milk ricotta, but you can use any kind you like, as long as it is fresh and high quality.

Roll and shape the gnocchi according to the instructions in the Gnocchi di Ricotta Master Dough recipe (page 46). Use the finished gnocchi in the following recipes.

RICOTTA

GNOCCHI DI RICOTTA ALLA BOSCAIOLA

RICOTTA DUMPLINGS WITH PANCETTA, MUSHROOMS, AND HERBS

Alla boscaiola means "in the style of the woodsman" and variations are found all over Italy; there are even Italian-American versions, most of which feature tomato sauce. Considering that the forests outside Bologna are rife with mushrooms, especially in fall, this is the perfect dish for that time of year. A lot of people ask me why I omit heavy cream, a common ingredient. The reason is to highlight the mushrooms and herbs, which evoke the aromas of the forest floor.

I prefer to use a mix of mushrooms for their different textures and flavors. This is easy to do because my trusted local forager goes out and gets me the craziest stuff. But you can modify the types of mushrooms you use based on the season and your location. Opt for a mix of button mushrooms, cremini, or whatever you find, or use just one type. The total amount should be 15 oz [425 g]. (Frozen porcini are fine, too. Before using, defrost completely, overnight in the refrigerator, uncovered on an absorbent non-terry cloth kitchen towel.)

You want to make the most of the mushroom's meaty texture, so don't slice them too thinly. Halve smaller mushrooms, quarter any that are medium in size, and cut larger ones into finger-thick slices.

SERVES 6

2 TBSP UNSALTED BUTTER

1 OZ [28 G] PANCETTA, CUT INTO ¼ IN [6 MM] BATONS

1 SMALL SHALLOT, THINLY SLICED

3 OZ [85 G] PORCINI MUSHROOMS, SLICED

3 OZ [85 G] CHANTERELLES, SLICED

3 OZ [85 G] KING TRUMPET MUSHROOMS, SLICED

3 OZ [85 G] OVOLI, SLICED

3 OZ [85 G] MORELS, SLICED

1 GARLIC CLOVE, SMASHED

1 SPRIG ROSEMARY

½ CUP [120 ML] DRY WHITE WINE

1 CUP [240 ML] BRODO DI FUNGHI (PAGE 246)

KOSHER SALT

1 RECIPE GNOCCHI DI RICOTTA (PAGE 46)

2 TBSP CHOPPED FRESH FLAT-LEAF PARSLEY

1 CUP [100 G] FINELY GRATED PARMIGIANO-REGGIANO

In a large sauté pan or skillet over medium-high heat, heat 1 Tbsp of the butter until frothy and golden. Add the pancetta and cook until crispy and the fat has rendered, about 2 minutes. Add the shallot and cook until it just begins to take color, about 2 minutes.

Add the mushrooms in order of density. First, the porcini mushrooms; cook for 30 seconds. Next, in this order, the chanterelles, king trumpet, ovoli, and morels, cooking for 20 seconds after each addition. Once all the mushrooms have been added, cook, without stirring or agitating the pan, for 1 minute more.

Add the garlic and rosemary and cook until fragrant, about 30 seconds. Add the wine and cook until the liquid in the pan has evaporated, about 40 seconds. Add the *brodo*, swirl the pan, and cook until the liquid has reduced by half, about 4 minutes. Add the remaining 1 Tbsp butter and swirl to melt. Remove and discard the garlic and rosemary. Set the sauce aside.

Bring a large pot of water to a rolling boil over high heat. Season the water with salt (see page 25). When the salt dissolves, add the gnocchi and cook until tender, 2 to 2½ minutes.

Meanwhile, return the sauce to medium heat and stir in the parsley. Using a spider, transfer the pasta to the sauce and gently swirl to coat. Add some pasta cooking water, as needed, to loosen the sauce. Serve immediately with the Parmigiano-Reggiano sprinkled on top.

BRODO DI FUNGHI

MUSHROOM BROTH

Mushroom broth brings a pleasant, subtle earthiness to recipes and it enhances the flavor of dishes featuring mushrooms. This recipe makes 2 qt [1.9 L] so you'll have plenty left over. Use it to simmer mushrooms for a side dish, to add to a vegetable minestrone, to cook polenta, or however else you like. Add scraps from mushroom trimmings from other recipes in this book, if you have them.

MAKES ABOUT 1 QT [.95 L]

½ LB [227 G] FRESH BUTTON MUSHROOMS, OR 1 OZ [28 G] DRIED PORCINI

2 TBSP UNSALTED BUTTER

1 GARLIC CLOVE, SMASHED

2 SPRIGS MARJORAM

½ CUP [120 ML] DRY WHITE WINE

1.5 QT/6 CUPS [1.4 L] COLD WATER

In a large bowl, smash the mushrooms with a whisk or potato masher to the size of peas and set aside.

In a large heavy-bottomed pot over high heat, melt the butter until frothy and golden. Add the garlic and marjoram and cook until aromatic, about 30 seconds. Add the smashed mushrooms and cook until their liquid is reduced by half, about 4 minutes. Add the wine, bring to a boil, and cook until the pan is almost dry, about 4 minutes.

Add the cold water and bring to a boil. Turn the heat to a low simmer and cook until the liquid is deep brown, about 1 hour. Strain the mixture through a fine-mesh sieve or chinois, pressing on the mushrooms with a ladle to extract any remaining liquid. Use now or cool the broth completely over an ice bath and refrigerate for later use.

The broth will keep, refrigerated in an airtight container, for up to 5 days or frozen for up to 6 months.

CRESCENTINE

To say the cuisine of Emilia-Romagna is cholesterol heavy would be putting it lightly. It embraces the use of *strutto* in the most wonderful ways. Indeed, there's an entire category of *strutto*-based breads. The exact recipes and names vary from town to town, but they include *piadine* (tortilla-like flatbreads cooked on a terra cotta surface heated over a fire), *tigelle* (disks of flattened dough made in a hinged press), the Gnocco Fritto (page 252), and, my favorite, *crescentine* (dough disks, squares, or diamonds deep-fried in *strutto*).

Crescentine are delicious on their own, but are especially good straight from the fryer draped with thinly sliced prosciutto (see page 250) or mortadella (see page 118), which warms beautifully from the heat. Serve either version as a starter before any of the pasta dishes in this book.

MAKES 25 TO 30 CRESCENTINE, SERVING 6

600 G [1 LB, 5 OZ] "00" FLOUR, PLUS MORE FOR DUSTING

530 G [1 LB, 2¾ OZ] STRUTTO

180 G [ABOUT 6⅓ OZ] WHOLE MILK

180 G [ABOUT 6⅓ OZ] WATER

10 G [ABOUT ⅓ OZ] FRESH YEAST

10 G [ABOUT ⅓ OZ] KOSHER SALT, PLUS MORE FOR SERVING

In the bowl of a stand mixer fitted with the dough hook, combine the flour and 80 g [about 2¾ oz] of *strutto*. Mix on low speed until thoroughly combined, about 2 minutes. Add the milk, water, and yeast and mix for 2 minutes more. Add the salt and mix for 4 minutes more, or until the dough is supple and elastic.

Lightly dust a work surface with flour. Turn the dough out onto the prepared surface and knead until completely smooth, about 3 minutes. Wrap the dough tightly in plastic wrap and refrigerate for at least 2 hours, and up to 48 hours.

Unwrap the dough and halve it using a bench scraper or sharp knife. Lightly flour your work surface. Roll out each dough half as you would roll out a *sfoglia* (see page 50) to a thickness of 20 Post-it® Notes. Using a straight edge or fluted cutter, cut the *sfoglia* into 3 by 2 in [7.5 by 5 cm] diamonds; other similarly sized shapes are fine, too.

Have a wire rack ready or line a platter with paper towels and set aside. In a medium high-sided pot over medium heat, heat the remaining *strutto* to 350°F [180°C]. Working in batches so as not to crowd the pan, fry the shaped dough until golden, 2 to 3 minutes, gently stirring and turning the pieces as they cook. Using a spider, transfer the *crescentine* to the rack or prepared platter. Season with salt and serve immediately. *Crescentine* do not keep well.

Going H.A.M. on Parma's Noble Cured Pork

To say I love prosciutto di Parma would be an understatement. When I lived in Bologna my diet was so prosciutto di Parma–heavy I suffered from salt headaches. (Worth it, by the way.) This cured pork haunch is so special to me I even had the ham's logo—the word "PARMA" topped with a crown—tattooed on my left forearm, a fact that delights my buddies in Emilia-Romagna to no end. Though there are many kinds of prosciutto in Italy—San Daniele, Cinta Senese, Norcia, and so on—the Parma version is the one I treasure most because it's sweet, savory, and soft.

Prosciutto di Parma isn't just the name for a type of air-cured ham. It's a legally defined term that denotes a location and style of production. It holds DOP (*Denominazione di Origine Protetta*) status, which means its production is regulated and controlled by the government to prevent poor quality versions or imposters from being sold as the real thing. To be eligible for DOP status, the prosciutto must be made from the back haunches of pigs bred in Emilia-Romagna.

The process requirements are also very specific. The first step is to salt the cleaned, skin-on haunches. The muscle is then caked with dry sea salt, while the skin is smeared with a mixture of sea salt and water. Next, the legs are set aside to dry in chambers with 80 percent humidity at temperatures ranging from 34 to 39°F [1 to 4°C]. After one week, another salt layer is applied. (Salt is the only preservative permitted in the production of prosciutto di Parma.)

A little more than two weeks from the second salting, the hams are hung to dry in temperature-controlled rooms with 75 percent humidity. The drying process lasts anywhere from 60 to 90 days, depending on the progress, which is judged by experts.

Once ready, the hams are washed and hung to dry on wooden frames for 3 months. The slow-curing phase, which transpires in ventilated rooms, gives prosciutto di Parma its signature sweetness. Finally, the muscle is covered with a paste of salt and *strutto*, which prevents the ham from drying out, and the ham is hung in dark cellars for 1 to 3 years, measured from the initial salting. The resident prosciutto master decides the exact duration based on "tasting" the ham and judging its readiness. Rather than cutting it open, he inserts a sharpened bone into the meat, takes it out, and smells its aromas. A prosciutto master can use his nose to determine exactly when a ham is ready, and there is truly no substitute for the real deal.

Enjoy it thinly sliced and eaten as is, or draped across melon, figs, or my favorite pre-pasta starters, Crescentine (page 248) and Gnocco Fritto (page 252). Lay it over veal to make *saltimbocca*. It can also be diced and used in pasta sauces, stuffings, or savory baked goods. Look for prosciutto di Parma at quality charcuterie shops and specialty foods stores and be sure the ham is stamped with the trademark logo. Unfortunately, there are lots of inferior hams out there that are easily mistaken or incorrectly marketed as the real deal.

GNOCCHI DI RICOTTA CON FONDUTA DI ROBIOLA E LARDO

RICOTTA DUMPLINGS WITH ROBIOLA AND CURED FATBACK

In Bologna, this dish is dubbed gnocchi *alla bava*, "drool-inducing gnocchi"—a nod to its deliciousness. For something so monochromatic as melted fat on cream sauce–drenched dumplings sprinkled with Parmigiano-Reggiano, it's hardly one-note. *Robiola* is a really bright and acidic cheese that distracts—in a good way–from the fattiness of the *lardo*. The dish is also super easy and quick to put together.

SERVES 6

3 CUPS [720 ML] HEAVY CREAM

1 CUP [100 G] FINELY GRATED PARMIGIANO-REGGIANO

4 OZ [113.5 G] ROBIOLA

KOSHER SALT

1 RECIPE GNOCCHI DI RICOTTA (PAGE 46)

6 OZ [170 G] LARDO, THINLY SLICED

SMALL PINCH OF FRESHLY GROUND BLACK PEPPER

Preheat the oven to 350°F [180°C].

In a medium heavy-bottomed pot over medium-high heat, bring the cream to a simmer. Carefully transfer the hot cream to a blender and blend on high speed for 30 seconds to aerate. Add ½ cup [50 g] of Parmigiano-Reggiano and blend again on high speed until incorporated. Add the *robiola* and continue blending on high speed until incorporated. Season with salt and transfer the sauce to a large sauté pan or skillet and keep warm over low heat.

Bring a large pot of water to a rolling boil over high heat. Season the water with salt (see page 25). When the salt dissolves, add the gnocchi and cook until tender, 2 to 2½ minutes.

Using a spider, transfer the gnocchi to the sauce and stir gently to coat. Add some pasta cooking water, as needed, to loosen the sauce. Transfer the gnocchi to an oven-safe serving platter or gratin dish. Drape the *lardo* evenly over the gnocchi and bake just until the *lardo* is translucent, 30 to 45 seconds. Serve immediately with the remaining Parmigiano-Reggiano sprinkled on top.

The sauce will keep, refrigerated in an airtight container, for up to 5 days.

GNOCCO FRITTO

To make a *gnocco fritto*, the fried gnocchi snack made across Emilia-Romagna, simply follow the recipe for Gnocchi di Ricotta (page 46) and sift 1 Tbsp baking powder in with the flour. The classic *gnocco fritto* dough doesn't have ricotta in it, but frying Gnocchi di Ricotta dough creates a light twist on tradition. Roll the dough to a thickness of ¼ in [6 mm]. Using a fluted pastry cutter, cut the dough into 2 in [5 cm] diamonds. Working in batches, deep-fry the *gnocco* in *strutto* or sunflower oil, turning once, about 45 seconds per side. They will puff as they fry. Drain on paper towels and serve with prosciutto or mortadella draped on top.

GNOCCHI DI RICOTTA CON TARTUFO BIANCO

GNOCCHI WITH WHITE TRUFFLES

White truffles are rare occurrences in nature; they even have to be hunted by specially trained dogs (see page 225). Naturally, such a sought-after product fetches a pretty penny on the open market. Adding to their cachet, they are only in season for a brief time in fall. A white truffle serving 6 weighs about 1 oz [from 24 to 32 grams] and costs $75 to $100, but the expense is completely worth it if you can swing it. They lend an earthy, ethereal nature to the food and are best served with buttery dishes such as this one.

Look for white truffles at quality cheesemongers, gourmet food shops, and online at kingofmushrooms.com and foodsinseason.com. Store your truffles wrapped in an absorbent paper towel in a sealed container in the refrigerator for up to 10 days, depending on the quality and firmness of the truffle.

SERVES 6

6 TBSP [84 G] UNSALTED BUTTER, AT ROOM TEMPERATURE

1 WHITE TRUFFLE, ABOUT 1 OZ [24 TO 32 G]

KOSHER SALT

1 RECIPE GNOCCHI DI RICOTTA (PAGE 46)

1 CUP [100 G] FINELY GRATED PARMIGIANO-REGGIANO

Using a clean, firm bristle nailbrush or clean toothbrush, gently remove any dirt from the truffle. Place 4 Tbsp [56 g] of butter in a medium bowl. Using a microplane, grate the outside of the truffle (about ⅙ oz [5 g]) into the butter. Add a pinch of salt and, using a rubber spatula, mix thoroughly and set aside.

Bring a large pot of water to a rolling boil over high heat. Season the water with salt (see page 25). When the salt dissolves, add the gnocchi and cook until tender, 2 to 2½ minutes.

Meanwhile, in a large sauté pan or skillet over low heat, heat the remaining 2 Tbsp of butter. Add 5 oz [150 ml] of pasta cooking water and bring to a rapid simmer, cooking for about 2 minutes. Add the truffle butter and swirl to emulsify. Using a spider, transfer the pasta to the sauce and gently swirl to coat. Add some pasta cooking water, as needed, to loosen the sauce. Transfer to a warm platter and dust with Parmigiano-Reggiano. Shave the remaining truffle with a truffle shaver or mandoline over the pasta. Serve immediately.

RESOURCES

WHERE TO EAT, DRINK, AND SHOP IN BOLOGNA

All'Osteria Bottega

Via Santa Caterina, 51
40123 Bologna
facebook.com/Osteria-Bottega
A bastion of bolognese pasta and meat specialties, including a perfect lasagna and an incredible selection of artisan salumi.

Amerigo dal 1934

Via Guglielmo Marconi, 14/16
40053 Savigno
amerigo1934.it
This generations-old trattoria, B&B, and general store in Emilia-Romagna's truffle capital is well worth the 40-minute drive from Bologna.

Antica Aguzzeria del Cavallo

Via Drapperie, 12B
40124 Bologna
aguzzeriadelcavallo.it
Antica Aguzzeria del Cavallo has been selling the most beautiful handcrafted brass pasta tools and kitchen implements since 1783.

Caffè Terzi

Via Guglielmo Oberdan, 10/d
40126 Bologna
caffeterzi.it
You can choose your preferred bean for espresso or cappuccino at this elegant coffee shop.

Enoteca Storica Faccioli

Via Altabella, 15/B
40126 Bologna
enotecastoricafaccioli.it
This organic, biodynamic, and natural wine bar is by far Bologna's best place to drink domestic and imported vino.

Il Pollaio

Mercato Albani
Via Francesco Albani
40129 Bologna
facebook.com/
IL-Pollaio-2079245282298386/
This former poultry shop in the Mercato Albani serves simple snacks and natural wines.

Le Golosità di Nonna Aurora

Via Aristotile Fioravanti, 45B
40129 Bologna
facebook.com/pages/category/
Diner/Le-Golosità-di-Nonna-Au-
rora-179267688756478/
For comfort food like *passatelli in brodo*, tagliatelle *ripassate in padella*, and lasagna.

Osteria del Mirasole

Via Giacomo Matteotti, 17
40017 San Giovanni in Persiceto
osteriadelmirasole.it
This trattoria in the countryside specializes in grilled meats and offers a delicious break from Bologna's many braises.

Pezzoli Enologia
Via Santo Stefano, 7
40125 Bologna
pezzolienologia.it
Go for the brass pasta tools, stay
for the huge selection of wine- and
digestif-making tools.

Ristorante Biagi
Via Saragozza, 65
40123 Bologna
ristorantebiagi1937.com
My go-to for bolognese comfort food
like *passatelli* and tortellini *in brodo*.

Trattoria di Via Serra
Via Luigi Serra, 9
40129 Bologna
trattoriadiviaserra.it
This trattoria just north of Bologna's main
train station is an institution dedicated
to serving locals. In fact, you'll probably
need one of them to make your booking
since they set aside so many tables for
regulars.

Vâgh íñ Ufézzí
Via de' Coltelli 9C
40124 Bologna
vaghinufezzi.it
A homey trattoria undiscovered by tour-
ists and serving just 6 to 8 dishes nightly.
The *balanzoni* are out of this world.

Vecchia Scuola Bolognese
Via Stalingrado, 81
40128 Bologna
vsb-bologna.it
Maestra Alessandra's cooking school
and casual lunchtime trattoria set in
Bologna's fairgrounds.

Vineria Favalli
Via Santo Stefano, 5A
40125 Bologna
facebook.com/vineriafavalli
This wine bar pours traditional and
organic wines from Italy and beyond.

WHERE TO EAT, DRINK, AND SHOP IN THE U.S.

Antico Molino Caputo
201-368-9197
caputoflour.com
A solid choice for pasta flour for home cooks and professionals alike.

Bellwether Farms
707-763-0993
bellwetherfarms.com
Ricotta and other dairy products made in Sonoma County.

Buon' Italia
212-633-9090
buonitalia.com
Flours, cheeses, *lardo*, and assorted Italian specialties.

Caputo Brothers
717-739-1091
caputobrotherscreamery.com
Ricotta and other speciality Italian dairy products.

D'Artagnan
800-327-8246
dartagnan.com
Purveyors of specialty meats including duck, wild boar, and rabbit.

Di Bruno Brothers
215-531-5666
dibruno.com
Pecorino Romano, Parmigiano-Reggiano, Gorgonzola, sheep's milk ricotta, and other Italian cheeses.

Fante's Kitchen Shop
800-44-FANTE
fantes.com
Kitchen store with an extensive catalog of Italian artisan products and pasta tools.

Foods in Season
866-767-2464
foodsinseason.com
This family-owned wild food business forages for a stunning array of mushrooms throughout the year. They also source stellar meat from the U.S., Canada, and even Japan.

Formaggio Kitchen
888-212-3224
formaggiokitchen.com
Lardo, cheeses, and other specialty products.

Gustiamo
718-860-2949
gustiamo.com
This Bronx-based online retailer stocks all the best Italian tomatoes and specialty products you need in your pantry.

JB Prince
212-683-3553
jbprince.com
Kitchen equipment and pasta tools.

King Arthur Flour
800-827-6836
kingarthurflour.com
Quality flours.

Market Hall Foods

510-250-6006

markethallfoods.com

A wide range of Italian specialty products.

OXO

oxo.com

800-545-4411

Good, sturdy cooking and baking utensils.

Sur La Table

800-243-0852

surlatable.com

High-end cookwear, sturdy pots, and pasta tools.

Williams-Sonoma

877-812-6235

williams-sonoma.com

Cookware and assorted pasta tools.

Zingerman's

888-636-8162

zingermans.com

Lardo, cheeses, and a huge variety of Italian specialty products.

Bibliography

Capatti, Alberto and Montanari, Massimo. *La Cucina Italiana: Storia di Una Cultura*. Bari: Laterza, 2005.

Ferrari, Ambra. *Emilia In Bocca*. Palermo: Il Vespro, 1979.

Gosetti della Salda, Anna. *Le Ricette Regionali Italiane*. Milan: Solares, 2005.

Martini, Fosca. *Romagna In Bocca*. Palermo: Il Vespro, 1977.

Riley, Gillian. *The Oxford Companion to Italian Food*. Oxford: Oxford University Press, 2009.

Spisni, Alessandra. *Le Ricette della Vecchia Scuola Bolognese*. Bologna: Minerva Edizioni, 2011.

Zanini De Vita, Oretta. *Atlante dei Prodotti Tipici: La Pasta*. Roma: Agra Editrice, 2004.

ACKNOWLEDGMENTS

To my wife, Grace. You are forever foremost in my mind. Thank you for your compassion and infinite support and love. My father, Alex Funke, thank you for your mastery, for shooting the first 5,000 photos for this book, and for teaching me how to be a gentleman and a craftsman.

To my mom, Emily Funke, you are a beacon of patience and love.

My brothers and sister, Graham, Jens, Soph, and Andy Funke—thanks for your humor, sophomoric culinary preferences, and incessant fascination with useless information. I love you all.

Katie Parla, you are undeniably the greatest. Thank you for the laughs, your literary acumen, and love of torts in brods. To Eric Wolfinger (right), thank you for sharing your gift of light and capturing the soul of my pasta in your shots.

To Maestra Alessandra and Maestro Alessandro Spisni, I am eternally grateful for the traditions and technique you've both passed on to me. Thank you for teaching me that the harmony in my life lives within the *sfoglia*. Davide Occhi, thank you for the incomparable quality of your *mattarelli* and continuing in your father's footsteps.

My brother, Kosaku Kawamura, *arigato gozaimasu* for your devotion to this craft, your honesty, and friendship. Thank you Lee Hefter, Wolfgang Puck, Ari Rosenson, and the entire Spago Family for forging me and instilling in me the enduring principles that define excellence.

To Francine Arnone for telling me to go to culinary school instead of boot camp—thanks, Ma!

Rich Melman, thank you for your warm hospitality and for selflessly sharing your depth of knowledge about this business. Thank you Eileen Stringer and Mike Psaltis for your expertise and for shepherding me through this process. To Mike Gould, thank you for your candid advice, generosity, and for teaching me the importance of a good attorney. Todd, Ruth, and Steve, I am humbled by your understanding and forever grateful for your kindness.

Gab, Alex, Rob, and Tastemade Studios, thanks for the *buenos*, 120 km/h porchetta, *macchia* in the forest, and trunk fucking the pizza in Napoli. To Ben Hundreds, who keeps it fresh to death, thank you for the Friday afternoon traffic calls, your kindness, and for always listening. All love brother. And to Jon Buscemi who also keeps it fresh to death, thank you for your impeccable taste, ingenuity, and generosity. Thank you Lucas Mann for your invaluable insight and friendship. To Sam Kass, Jeff Dunn, and Gareth Asten at Acre for your astounding brainpower and for casting a wide net of support and encouragement. To Carson, claw on the ground wing in the sky. Thank you Nancy Silverton; you are the godmother. Forever grateful to Michele Forgione, my *fratello*, for your plethora of knowledge and selfless generosity. To Jon and Vinny, thank you for your friendship and for changing L.A. for the better—for all of us. Chris Bianco, you are the spiritual architect; thank you for your wisdom. To the day ones on the Bucato kill team—you know who you are WSVB: my gratitude for holding it down through it all. VANS, I love vans. Huge thank you to Danny "Hombre" Chavez for your quiet leadership and for testing all these recipes. To Louis and Big Tony, thank you for your focus and passion for excellence. *Grazie* to Aliza for the help on the set.

Thank you Janet and Gusto 54 for your vision and belief. My deepest gratitude to the extraordinary team at Felix: your dedication and talent are an inspiration to me every day. To Nunzia, Franca, Stefania, Paola, Sabina, Anna, and all the incredible women who have graciously helped me build my pasta lexicon, I am indebted to you forever.

Lastly, a heartfelt thank you to the entire team at Chronicle, especially Camaren Subhiyah, Vanessa Dina, Kathy Brennan, Leigh Saffold, Magnolia Molcan, Tera Killip, Steve Kim, Zaneta Jung, and Christine Carswell, for their patience and sharing their enthusiasm for this book.

Katie would like to thank her wonderful agent, Alison Fargis at Stonesong, for guidance and support. Thanks to Joj for managing travel logistics and generally tolerating my editing-induced stress. To my friend and host in Los Angeles, Sarni Rogers, I owe you a million pasta dishes. Hans Fama, your hospitality and patience were a gift. And to Evan Funke, your discipline inspired me every day.

INDEX

ABOUT THE AUTHORS

EVAN FUNKE is a two-time James Beard-nominated chef based in Los Angeles. After working for six years with Wolfgang Puck at the iconic Spago in Beverly Hills, Funke departed for Bologna where he apprenticed with master pasta maker Alessandra Spisni at La Vecchia Scuola Bolognese. Under Spisni's tutelage, Funke honed the time-honored techniques of making pasta by hand and acquired skills that would change his approach to cooking for good. Upon his return to the U.S., Funke took on the role of Executive Chef of Rustic Canyon in Santa Monica, where he solidified a "return to terroir" approach to cooking and cultivated enduring relationships with California's best farmers and ranchers. In 2013, Funke's Bucato opened to immediate critical acclaim as one of L.A.'s top restaurants and set a new standard for handmade pasta in the city. Felix, Funke's current venture, opened in 2017 and is a collaboration with Toronto-based restaurant group GUSTO54. Situated on famed Abbot Kinney Boulevard in Venice in L.A., critically-acclaimed Felix embodies Italian cooking sensibilities with a menu reflecting seasonality, expert craftsmanship, and genuine hospitality.

Funke was a semifinalist for James Beard "Rising Star Chef" at Rustic Canyon in 2009 and finalist for "Best New Restaurant" at Felix in 2018. FELIX continues to garner national recognition and was named to *Esquire*'s "Best New Restaurants in America 2017," Eater's "12 Best New Restaurants in America 2017," *Bon Appétit*'s "The Best Pasta We Ate in 2017," was short-listed for *Bon Appétit*'s "America's Best New Restaurants 2018", featured on Thrillist's "25 Best Italian Restaurants in America 2018" as well as the *Los Angeles Times* "101 Restaurants We Love 2018." The documentary *Funke* (Tastemade) chronicles Funke's journey to open Felix and debuted at the Los Angeles Film Festival in 2018.

KATIE PARLA, a New Jersey native, is a Rome-based food and beverage journalist, culinary guide, and educator. She is the creator of the *Saveur*-award–winning food and travel site KatieParla.com, the ebook *Eating & Drinking in Rome*, more than twenty travel guides, and co-author of the IACP award–winning cookbook *Tasting Rome*. Parla has appeared on and produced *Bizarre Foods* with Andrew Zimmern and *F*ck, That's Delicious* with Action Bronson, and served as a culinary concierge on Season 2 of Netflix's *Master of None*. Her travel writing, recipes, and food criticism have appeared in the *New York Times*, *Food & Wine*, *Saveur*, *Australian Gourmet Traveller*, the *Guardian*, *AFAR*, *Condé Nast Traveler*, *Punch*, *Eater*, and more. Her latest cookbook, *Food of the Italian South*, was published in 2019.

Chronicle Books publishes distinctive books and gifts. From award-winning children's titles, bestselling cookbooks, and eclectic pop culture to acclaimed works of art and design, stationery, and journals, we craft publishing that's instantly recognizable for its spirit and creativity. Enjoy our publishing and become part of our community at www.chroniclebooks.com.